To You and Your Awesomeness.

Let's Get Started

This *Year of Wow Daily Attraction Journal* reflects what I do on a regular basis to attract what I want. It's really powerful. Every time I would write in my day timer - I would write down exactly what you see here in this journal. I kept thinking - *I wish these categories were all written out already* and that's when I realized it was time to create this journal.

How it's laid out is that you will get the background explanation of what **QQCC** stands for and how you can use it to get unstuck, anytime AND attract the amazing life you deserve all at the same time!

Next, you'll see an example of how I use this process.

Then on to the heart of the Journal - the Overall Goals and Intentions for the Year - it's here that you want to chart your BIG IDEAS/GOALS/INTENTIONS. I would recommend dog-earring this page and coming back to it often to see if your daily focus is in alignment.

After that, you will see your daily journal sheets to use. Special review pages are at the 30, 60, 180, 300 day marks - these are good points to reflect on what you've accomplished, what you've been challenged with and perhaps are avoiding and then add to or make changes to your overall goals and intentions.

At the end of the book, we've given some information on how to connect with us. You're embarking on a life-changing journey and you don't need to go it alone. We're here for you to help in whatever way we can and at all kinds of different levels so you can create your **Year of Wow**!!

What's the Background?

Working with the Law of Attraction for over 15 years I am constantly finding new ways to implement the basics.

The bottom-line is that 'like attracts like' and if we want to have what we want in our life we must become more like it energetically.

Science tells us that when we observe something, we change it just by the act of observing. The problem with most of us is that we focus (observe) more often on what we don't want rather than what we do want. By focusing on what we don't want - we match that energy and therefore attract more of it.

What I have found through my work with my private clients is a simple formula called **QQCC**. So far, this process is the easiest way I could sift down the whole Attraction process to something that is easy to remember, usable in everyday life and highly effective.

As I mentioned, most of us get caught up in our day to day life and become focused on what is in front of us - usually a lack of what we truly want. Even though we set goals and have a true, burning desire - what will continue to show up is what we're focused on and what we're vibrating energetically.

That's where **QQCC** comes in. (Yes, I promise to fill you in on what that stands for!) **QQCC** will focus you on what you want AND also put you in an energetic match to what you want. Cool, hey?

Remember, the bottom-line is 'like attracts like' and you've already been doing it. With this Daily Journal you'll be now attracting more of what you DO want!

QQCC - What it Stands For

QQCC stands for - **Question**, **Questfirmation**, **Clear**, **Celebrate**. Each of these is a process you can implement.

In any moment where you want to change how you feel, what's happening or to get unstuck, remember **QQCC**. That's just how powerful these four processes can be in one's life.

Question
The way your mind works is that as soon as you ask a question, it goes to work to find an answer. We want to reform your way of asking questions so it works for you, not against you.

What do I mean by that? Typically, we will pose a question in our mind or even ask it aloud but the problem comes when we, ourselves, go about answering the question.
You need to stop that practice. Yes, it's what everyone does. Yes, it's what we all learned. No, it's not as effective as it what I'm about to share with you.

Instead, you want to ask your question and let your subconscious mind do the work. Ask a question and go do something else. This is called - 'getting out of your own way'.

When you ask a question and then try to come up with the answer - you are typically accessing only what you already know with your conscious mind. Even when you're Googling something, you'll only be able to see what already aligns with your preconceived ideas.

The most brilliant thinkers best ideas often came in times of rest, sleep or meditation - or while focused on something else entirely.

When you ask a question and don't immediately employ your conscious mind, your powerful subconscious mind goes to work scanning the environment for a match your question. I also believe it's in direct communication with Infinite Intelligence and that, my friend, is where your power to create explodes!

Questions like 'What Would it Take...?' (WWIT) or 'What/Who could show up...?' or 'How..?' are all good ways to start your questions. The important piece is that you ask without YOU trying to come up with an answer.

Next, after you ask your question, you go back to doing your work or you can go do something that is going to keep you preoccupied with something else. You can meditate, nap...whatever works but then your job is to pay attention to what thoughts or ideas pop to mind.

You'll start to get a sense that these ideas or thoughts are different - not coming from your regular process of 'figuring it out' but from somewhere else.

What I find is that this is a very subtle process most times and sometimes the ideas and thoughts just flow! More often than not the process is very subtle and you'll suddenly find yourself picking up a book that has the exact answer you were looking for but you might not even realize it right away.

Here's a few examples of how I've seen this work:

Question gets asked. Go sit on the deck to get some sun. A flood of ideas hits and you can't wait to get back and implement them.

Question gets asked multiple times. You're out shopping and decide to buy a magazine that somehow caught your eye - which is out of the ordinary for you. You read a fascinating article with really good ideas that you know you can use. A day later you realize that the ideas are exactly what you were asking for. (yes, it's easy to forget what you were asking for!! That's why this journal is great for reminding you!!)

A simple thought in the form of a question comes and goes - something like 'wouldn't it be interesting if this happened?'. Not long after, it happens.

Your Mission, Should You Choose to Accept It:

Ask a question. (if it's something you really want to change fast - ask it 20-30 times a day)

Go do something that doesn't involve you trying to figure out the answer to your question.

Pay attention to what bubbles up. This could be ideas, thoughts, inspiration - take action even if it doesn't make sense.

For the purposes of this journal - when you see this icon - write down your 'Ask' of the Universe for the day. What do you want help with? What would you like to accomplish? What would you like the Universe to handle?
What question would you like answered?
What problem would you most like to have solved?

Question

Ask
WWIT?

Do this daily and notice how things become easier, effortless.

Questfirmation

A Questfirmation (QF) is an affirmation in the form of a question. Maybe you've tried affirmations in the past, if you've had the same experience as me you will have found that affirmations do work....eventually.

Recently, I had been starting to post my affirmations in the form of a question and I suddenly had the inspiration of calling this a Questfirmation (QF). As I used QF's every day, I found that the attraction process was speeding up tremendously. I asked my clients to start using them and they found the same thing.

I form the QF in two parts: Why.....? How great is it....? Here's an example of what I think a lot of people would like to change:

Why was it so easy to double this month's income?
How great is it that it was so easy to double this month's income?

You'll notice that they are both said as if it's already happened. The desire is already done.

The reason QF's work is for much the same reason that questions work - they put your brain into the answer-finding mode. The difference is that, like an affirmation, you are presupposing that what you desire is already a reality.

With the 'Why' QF, you automatically put your brain into answer-finding mode. It HAS TO seek out how this happened. It's almost like the energy of doing this becomes a very powerful magnet which draws in ideas, solutions and synchronicities.

With the 'Why' QF it's like the brain looks at what your current reality is and then it looks at the desired reality and goes ' hmm, what the heck went on between these two realities to make this reality become that reality?' It has to find a solution to this challenge. What I find is that it's kind of like your computer, it's like a program working constantly in the background until a solution, idea or synchronicity makes it to the surface for your conscious mind to become aware of and act on.

Much like asking a question, as mentioned before, an idea, solution or synchronicity with bubble up for you to become aware of and take action on.

What I have found is that if you only ask 'Why' QF's, it can make you feel a little cranky because in the background, part of your brain is always aware that 'we're not there yet' - which, of course, it's trying to resolve.

That's why I found asking 'How great is it' QF's are also really necessary to the process because they put you into a very positive energetic state.

When you ask 'How great is it.....' QF's you're presupposing how actually awesome it is that what you want has happened - you put your energetic state into alignment with what you want. It's as if it's already done and you're celebrating it. You automatically are vibrating with it being a reality. How much quicker do you think you'll attract if you're in vibrational alignment with the object of your desire?

They key to this is actually allowing yourself to get into that elevated state of happiness or excitement or joy of having what you want in your life! The more you can do this, the more you magnetize and draw the ideas, solutions and synchronicities to you.

Your Mission, Should You Choose to Accept It:

For everything you want to have, be or do in your life, create a Questfirmation about it.

Throughout the day - ask your QF's. Ask the 'Why' QF's first and then the 'How great is it' QF's next.

You can also do the same in the moment when you want something to shift or get unstuck. You'll notice that you'll experience frustration much less.

Questfirmation

Affirm

Why? How?

For the purposes of the Journal - when you see this icon - write out your QF's for the day. I usually just write one statement for one desire and then I mentally or out loud just plug in the Why before the statement and then the How great is it?

Here's some examples:

~ my sales increased exponentially?

Then I'll do my QF's:
Why did my sales increase exponentially?
How great is it that my sales increased exponentially?

~ found the love of my life?
QF's:
Why was it so easy to find the love of my life?
How great is it that I found the love of my life?

~ easily paid off my debt
QF's:
Why was it so easy to pay off all my debt?
How great is it that I paid off all my debt?

Get the hang of it?

Now I could give you a lot more information here but this should get you going. You will be able to find more about Questfirmations at **AttractMoreNow.com** or in one of my Questfirmation books where I will go into more detail and give you tons of different Questfirmations you can use for specific topics.

Clear

Energy gets stuck in our vibrational/energy field. An incident, a conclusion, an unkind word, someone else's energy - any of these (and more) can get stuck and block our forward flow.

It's important to move out any blocks because they slow down your attraction process. You'll know you have a block if you've tried everything by the book and you still don't seem to make any headway.

There are all kinds of theories and modalities that people use to move this energy out of your field from acupuncture to reiki to hypnosis to therapy and all of them can work.

I'm all about ease and efficiency because I know that if it ain't easy - people won't do it.

Over the past few years I have come across a number of people using clearing statements that move that energy just through the process of saying the statement. I started using it for myself and my clients and the results were astonishing!! All of a sudden, my clients were shifting into much higher states of attraction and we were able to clear out long-standing beliefs (conscious and sub-conscious). Money blocks suddenly cleared and people were making more money, more easily. Family issues were suddenly not issues anymore. Attracting the wrong type of people suddenly turned into finding soul mates.

I started asking the question 'is there an even easier clearing I can use with my clients that will create profound results?' Not long after , an idea bubbled up and then another. I started using my own clearing statement with my private clients and the same amazing results continued to happen!

How does it work? I haven't a clue.

All I do know is that it works when people are open to receiving the energy of the clearing. What it seems to do is eliminate the limiting belief or negative feeling at its core.

I do talk more about this in the **AttractMoreNow Essentials**, **Attraction Mindset** and **Quantum Blockbusting** programs, if you're interested to find out more.

In the meantime, I'm hoping you'll be open to trying it out. It truly has been one of the most profound life-shifting tools I have ever used personally and with my clients.

Curious? Here's the clearing statement:

De-story, Transform, Release.

Here's what it means:

De-story - for every limiting belief and negative feeling we have - there is at least one story that locks it into place. Having a story (or conclusion, or belief, or thought) about anything immediately limits our possibilities. With the addition of de-story to the clearing statement - what we're doing is eliminating the story at its root - wherever it started. Wherever you adopted that story, belief or thought - we're taking the energy of it and changing it.

Transform - because we're dealing with energy and it can neither be created nor destroyed - what we need to do with the energy of this limiting belief is transform it. So we are de-storying it and transforming the energy of it into something open to all possibilities and more positive.

Release - Now we want to take that old energy of the limiting belief and let it go out of your field and back out into the Universe. Because we're transforming the energy of the old story that old energy won't be attracted to you again and stick in your field unless you choose to adopt that limiting belief again.

Cool, hey?

Now there are **two other things** that you need to know about the clearing statement.

The Set up - This is where you identify the limiting belief or negative feeling you want to eliminate.

For example - you could start with this:

Everywhere I took on this limiting belief, am I willing to destroy and uncreate it? (you then say 'yes' to yourself) Then you would say - De-story, Transform, Release.

*(For clearings on every topic you can possibly imagine, and to experience these clearings directly with me - try out the **AttractMoreNow Essentials** Free Trial.)*

The After-Experience - most everyone will experience one of these three things after they receive the Clearing Statement.

Nothing - Some people experience nothing after they have received the statement. Nothing comes to mind, they don't feel anything (this happens to my husband Geoff when I clear him) BUT the limiting belief or negative feeling changes.

They may not experience it til later but what they'll find is that they will take different action as a result in having the shift in the belief/feeling.

Thought/Image - Some people will have a thought or image pop to mind. It may or may not seem related to the belief or feeling being cleared on but you want to explore it and clear on it unless it's a really positive, light feeling.

If you clear on the thought or image and something else pops to mind - keep clearing until it does feel really light.

Feeling - Some people will experience a feeling in their body after they receive the Clearing Statement. This can be ANY KIND of feeling from feeling tingly to feeling light-headed to even having some pain or heaviness in parts of your body. It's all okay - just notice it - be light with it and keep clearing on it until it feels light and or good.   What's happening is that you're changing your beliefs/feelings at a cellular level. You are actually changing the consciousness of your body and doing a re-set.

Wild, huh?

Your Mission, Should You Choose to Accept It:

Whenever you notice a limiting belief or negative feeling - clear on it.

Throughout the day - if you find yourself getting wound up about something or worrying or having any limiting belief or negative feeling - just do the clearing process. If anything, it will shift your focus long enough to let the energy go of the moment.

You can also do the same in the moment when you want something to shift or get unstuck. You'll notice that you'll experience frustration much less.

For the purposes of the Journal - when you see this icon - notice if any of your Questions or Questfirmations have brought up any limiting belief or negative feelings or heavy feelings in your body.

Clear

Activate

De-Story, Transform
Release

Write down what you're noticing and clear on it.
Keep clearing on it until you feel lighter or at least neutral.

Celebrate

When we celebrate we bring ourselves back into the present moment. It is in the present moment that we have access to all of our power.

When I say 'celebrate', I mean do a happy dance, pat yourself on the back , be excited about what you've created. I also mean that you shift into appreciation or gratitude. Doing any one of these things will immediately get you unstuck from any situation.

It will do this by shifting your focus and your energy which allows you to come back into the present moment and puts you into a more open, more positive state of awareness. This automatically elevates your vibration and starts to align you with what you desire.

Celebration, appreciation and gratitude also help you to acknowledge your creations.

The easiest thing we do as humans is focus on the negatives and forget about all the positives. It's just the way our brain is wired. That's why people have a hard time with Law of Attraction because they're always wondering if it's working and rarely acknowledging all that they've created through attraction.

You ARE a powerful creator - now it's time to Celebrate it!!

Your Mission, Should You Choose to Accept It:

For everything you have, be and do in your life, Celebrate it! (Yes, I did intentionally write everything be Be! You are always Being something in every moment.)

Throughout the day - celebrate your accomplishments. Celebrate the good, the bad and the ugly which means, you're creating it all - so celebrate your create and if it's bad or ugly - decide from that moment that you're a powerful creator and that you are now going to choose something better!

You can also do the same in the moment when you want something to shift or get unstuck. Celebrate, appreciate or be grateful - you'll notice that you'll experience an immediate shift.

For the purposes of the Journal - when you see this icon - write 10 accomplishments, creations or things to be grateful for.

What you'll start to notice is how you asked for something and that it showed up.

What Energy Can I Be?

Remember, it's all about energy, right? We can choose what energy or state we need to be to accomplish what we want. I usually just ask this question and I'll get one or two words like - Strategic, Fun, Focused, Happy, Silly, Open as examples. Just ask the question and see what words or phrases bubble up for you. Whatever it is - it's right - don't second-guess yourself!

Then just remind yourself throughout the day to be that energy.

Alright, have fun!! Enjoy the process, be light about it and know that whatever is coming up or happening is perfect!!

This IS YOUR YEAR OF WOW!!!!

Remember, you can always connect with us if you have any questions - just go over to AttractMoreNow.com and once in you're in the site you'll find my contact information. You might want to go there now and bookmark it - lol.

You can always connect on Facebook, Facebook.com/KarenLuniw or Facebook.com/AttractMoreNow

No matter what - remember that we are here for you to help you achieve the amazing life you deserve!!

How to Use this Journal

Here's an example of how I would fill out this journal - of course fill it out the way it works best for you - just thought I'd give you an insight on how I make this work for me.

More details about what to put in each area is coming up next!

1: February 15th, 2014

Today I'd like help with:
Being super-productive
Having a fun day
WWIT to reach more ppl?
WWIT to double today's sales?

Questfirmations: Why? How?
- such a great day?
- connected with 100 ppl today?
- doubled my income today?

Any Thoughts. Feelings. Images Coming Up?
I won't have enough time
Am I crazy, is this impossible?
Am I asking for too much?

Celebrate 10 Things! What Showed Up?
Finished project! Car is working better!
Surprise from Geoff! New Subscribers!
My pooches. Sunny day. Great sleep.
Call from Joanne! Great client breakthru!
My cool phone.

What Energy can I Be Today?

Abundance can be had simply by consciously receiving what already has been given. ~ Sufi saying

Overall Goals for the Year

Take a brief look back one year from today - what did you want to change that hasn't yet changed?

Now, imagine it's one year from today - what are the 3-5 areas you would like to see significant changes in?

Write those down here and also write down Questfirmations for each. Those are going to your over-arching focus every day. Dog-ear this page and keep referring back to it to remind yourself what you're committed to for the year.

Overall Goals for the Year

1:

Question

Ask
WWIT?

Today I'd like help with:

Questfirmation

Affirm
Why? How?

Questfirmations: Why? How?

Clear

Activate
De-Story, Transform
Release

Any Thoughts, Feelings, Images Coming Up?

Celebrate

Appreciate
Woohooo!!

Celebrate 10 Things! What Showed Up?

What Energy can I Be Today?

*Abundance can be had simply by consciously receiving
what already has been given. ~ Sufi saying*

2:

Question

Ask

WWIT?

Today I'd like help with:

Questfirmation

Affirm

Why? How?

Questfirmations: Why? How?

Clear

Activate

De-Story, Transform Release

Any Thoughts, Feelings, Images Coming Up?

Celebrate

Appreciate

Woohooo!!

Celebrate 10 Things! What Showed Up?

What Energy can I Be Today?

3:

Question

Ask

WWIT?

Today I'd like help with:

Questfirmation

Affirm

Why? How?

Questfirmations: Why? How?

Clear

Activate

De-Story, Transform Release

Any Thoughts, Feelings, Images Coming Up?

Celebrate

Appreciate

Woohooo!!

Celebrate 10 Things! What Showed Up?

What Energy can I Be Today?

4:

Question

Ask

WWIT?

Today I'd like help with:

Questfirmation

Affirm

Why? How?

Questfirmations: Why? How?

Clear

Activate

De-Story, Transform Release

Any Thoughts, Feelings, Images Coming Up?

Celebrate

Appreciate

Woohooo!!

Celebrate 10 Things! What Showed Up?

What Energy can I Be Today?

5:

Question

Ask

WWIT?

Today I'd like help with:

Questfirmation

Affirm

Why? How?

Questfirmations: Why? How?

Clear

Activate

De-Story, Transform
Release

Any Thoughts, Feelings, Images Coming Up?

Celebrate

Appreciate

Woohooo!!

Celebrate 10 Things! What Showed Up?

What Energy can I Be Today?

6:

Question

Ask

WWIT?

Today I'd like help with:

Questfirmation

Affirm

Why? How?

Questfirmations: Why? How?

Clear

Activate

De-Story, Transform Release

Any Thoughts, Feelings, Images Coming Up?

Celebrate

Appreciate

Woohooo!!

Celebrate 10 Things! What Showed Up?

What Energy can I Be Today?

7:

Question

Ask

WWIT?

Today I'd like help with:

Questfirmation

Affirm

Why? How?

Questfirmations: Why? How?

Clear

Activate

De-Story, Transform Release

Any Thoughts, Feelings, Images Coming Up?

Celebrate

Appreciate

Woohooo!!

Celebrate 10 Things! What Showed Up?

What Energy can I Be Today?

8:

Question

Ask

WWIT?

Today I'd like help with:

Questfirmation

Affirm

Why? How?

Questfirmations: Why? How?

Clear

Activate

De-Story, Transform Release

Any Thoughts, Feelings, Images Coming Up?

Celebrate

Appreciate

Woohooo!!

Celebrate 10 Things! What Showed Up?

What Energy can I Be Today?

9:

Question

Ask

WWIT?

Today I'd like help with:

Questfirmation

Affirm

Why? How?

Questfirmations: Why? How?

Clear

Activate

De-Story, Transform Release

Any Thoughts, Feelings, Images Coming Up?

Celebrate

Appreciate

Woohooo!!

Celebrate 10 Things! What Showed Up?

What Energy can I Be Today?

10:

Question

Ask

WWIT?

Today I'd like help with:

Questfirmation

Affirm

Why? How?

Questfirmations: Why? How?

Clear

Activate

De-Story, Transform Release

Any Thoughts, Feelings, Images Coming Up?

Celebrate

Appreciate

Woohooo!!

Celebrate 10 Things! What Showed Up?

What Energy can I Be Today?

11:

Question

Ask

WWIT?

Today I'd like help with:

Questfirmation

Affirm

Why? How?

Questfirmations: Why? How?

Clear

Activate

De-Story, Transform Release

Any Thoughts, Feelings, Images Coming Up?

Celebrate

Appreciate

Woohooo!!

Celebrate 10 Things! What Showed Up?

What Energy can I Be Today?

12:

Question

Ask

WWIT?

Today I'd like help with:

Questfirmation

Affirm

Why? How?

Questfirmations: Why? How?

Clear

Activate

De-Story, Transform Release

Any Thoughts, Feelings, Images Coming Up?

Celebrate

Appreciate

Woohooo!!

Celebrate 10 Things! What Showed Up?

What Energy can I Be Today?

13:

Ask

WWIT?

Today I'd like help with:

Questfirmation

Affirm

Why? How?

Questfirmations: Why? How?

Clear

Activate

De-Story, Transform Release

Any Thoughts, Feelings, Images Coming Up?

Celebrate

Appreciate

Woohooo!!

Celebrate 10 Things! What Showed Up?

What Energy can I Be Today?

14:

Question

Ask

WWIT?

Today I'd like help with:

Questfirmation

Affirm

Why? How?

Questfirmations: Why? How?

Clear

Activate

De-Story, Transform Release

Any Thoughts, Feelings, Images Coming Up?

Celebrate

Appreciate

Woohooo!!

Celebrate 10 Things! What Showed Up?

What Energy can I Be Today?

15:

Question

Ask

WWIT?

Today I'd like help with:

Questfirmation

Affirm

Why? How?

Questfirmations: Why? How?

Clear

Activate

De-Story, Transform Release

Any Thoughts, Feelings, Images Coming Up?

Celebrate

Appreciate

Woohooo!!

Celebrate 10 Things! What Showed Up?

What Energy can I Be Today?

16:

Ask

WWIT?

Today I'd like help with:

Affirm

Why? How?

Questfirmations: Why? How?

Activate

De-Story, Transform Release

Any Thoughts, Feelings, Images Coming Up?

Appreciate

Woohooo!!

Celebrate 10 Things! What Showed Up?

What Energy can I Be Today?

17:

Question

Ask

WWIT?

Today I'd like help with:

Questfirmation

Affirm

Why? How?

Questfirmations: Why? How?

Clear

Activate

De-Story, Transform
Release

Any Thoughts, Feelings, Images Coming Up?

Celebrate

Appreciate

Woohooo!!

Celebrate 10 Things! What Showed Up?

What Energy can I Be Today?

18:

Question

Ask
WWIT?

Today I'd like help with:

Questfirmation

Affirm
Why? How?

Questfirmations: Why? How?

Clear

Activate
De-Story, Transform Release

Any Thoughts, Feelings, Images Coming Up?

Celebrate

Appreciate
Woohooo!!

Celebrate 10 Things! What Showed Up?

What Energy can I Be Today?

19:

Question

Ask

WWIT?

Today I'd like help with:

Questfirmation

Affirm

Why? How?

Questfirmations: Why? How?

Clear

Activate

De-Story, Transform Release

Any Thoughts, Feelings, Images Coming Up?

Celebrate

Appreciate

Woohooo!!

Celebrate 10 Things! What Showed Up?

What Energy can I Be Today?

20:

Question

Ask

WWIT?

Today I'd like help with:

Questfirmation

Affirm

Why? How?

Questfirmations: Why? How?

Clear

Activate

De-Story, Transform Release

Any Thoughts, Feelings, Images Coming Up?

Celebrate

Appreciate

Woohooo!!

Celebrate 10 Things! What Showed Up?

What Energy can I Be Today?

21:

Question

Ask
WWIT?

Today I'd like help with:

Questfirmation

Affirm
Why? How?

Questfirmations: Why? How?

Clear

Activate
De-Story, Transform
Release

Any Thoughts, Feelings, Images Coming Up?

Celebrate

Appreciate
Woohooo!!

Celebrate 10 Things! What Showed Up?

What Energy can I Be Today?

22:

Question

Ask
WWIT?

Today I'd like help with:

Questfirmation

Affirm
Why? How?

Questfirmations: Why? How?

Clear

Activate
De-Story, Transform
Release

Any Thoughts, Feelings, Images Coming Up?

Celebrate

Appreciate
Woohooo!!

Celebrate 10 Things! What Showed Up?

What Energy can I Be Today?

23:

Question

Ask
WWIT?

Today I'd like help with:

Questfirmation

Affirm
Why? How?

Questfirmations: Why? How?

Clear

Activate
De-Story, Transform
Release

Any Thoughts, Feelings, Images Coming Up?

Celebrate

Appreciate
Woohooo!!

Celebrate 10 Things! What Showed Up?

What Energy can I Be Today?

24:

Question

Ask
WWIT?

Today I'd like help with:

Questfirmation

Affirm
Why? How?

Questfirmations: Why? How?

Clear

Activate
De-Story, Transform
Release

Any Thoughts, Feelings, Images Coming Up?

Celebrate

Appreciate
Woohooo!!

Celebrate 10 Things! What Showed Up?

What Energy can I Be Today?

25:

Question

Ask

WWIT?

Today I'd like help with:

Questfirmation

Affirm

Why? How?

Questfirmations: Why? How?

Clear

Activate

De-Story, Transform Release

Any Thoughts, Feelings, Images Coming Up?

Celebrate

Appreciate

Woohooo!!

Celebrate 10 Things! What Showed Up?

What Energy can I Be Today?

26:

Question

Ask

WWIT?

Today I'd like help with:

Questfirmation

Affirm

Why? How?

Questfirmations: Why? How?

Clear

Activate

De-Story, Transform Release

Any Thoughts, Feelings, Images Coming Up?

Celebrate

Appreciate

Woohooo!!

Celebrate 10 Things! What Showed Up?

What Energy can I Be Today?

27:

Question — Today I'd like help with:

Ask

WWIT?

Questfirmation — Questfirmations: Why? How?

Affirm

Why? How?

Clear — Any Thoughts, Feelings, Images Coming Up?

Activate

De-Story, Transform Release

Celebrate — Celebrate 10 Things! What Showed Up?

Appreciate

Woohooo!!

What Energy can I Be Today?

28:

Question

Ask
WWIT?

Today I'd like help with:

Questfirmation

Affirm
Why? How?

Questfirmations: Why? How?

Clear

Activate
De-Story, Transform Release

Any Thoughts, Feelings, Images Coming Up?

Celebrate

Appreciate
Woohooo!!

Celebrate 10 Things! What Showed Up?

What Energy can I Be Today?

29:

Question

Ask

WWIT?

Today I'd like help with:

Questfirmation

Affirm

Why? How?

Questfirmations: Why? How?

Clear

Activate

De-Story, Transform Release

Any Thoughts, Feelings, Images Coming Up?

Celebrate

Appreciate

Woohooo!!

Celebrate 10 Things! What Showed Up?

What Energy can I Be Today?

30:

Question

Ask

WWIT?

Today I'd like help with:

Questfirmation

Affirm

Why? How?

Questfirmations: Why? How?

Clear

Activate

De-Story, Transform Release

Any Thoughts, Feelings, Images Coming Up?

Celebrate

Appreciate

Woohooo!!

Celebrate 10 Things! What Showed Up?

What Energy can I Be Today?

What Changes Have You Noticed?

Okay, we're 30 days in - what's changed? Review your Overall
Goals - are you noticing changes yet? Do your goals need to be
updated?

What, if anything, needs to be changed or added to your process?
Write down your thoughts here.?

31:

Question

Ask

WWIT?

Today I'd like help with:

Questfirmation

Affirm

Why? How?

Questfirmations: Why? How?

Clear

Activate

De-Story, Transform
Release

Any Thoughts, Feelings, Images Coming Up?

Celebrate

Appreciate

Woohooo!!

Celebrate 10 Things! What Showed Up?

What Energy can I Be Today?

32:

Question

Ask

WWIT?

Today I'd like help with:

Questfirmation

Affirm

Why? How?

Questfirmations: Why? How?

Clear

Activate

De-Story, Transform Release

Any Thoughts, Feelings, Images Coming Up?

Celebrate

Appreciate

Woohooo!!

Celebrate 10 Things! What Showed Up?

What Energy can I Be Today?

33:

Ask

WWIT?

Today I'd like help with:

Questfirmation

Affirm

Why? How?

Questfirmations: Why? How?

Clear

Activate

De-Story, Transform Release

Any Thoughts, Feelings, Images Coming Up?

Celebrate

Appreciate

Woohooo!!

Celebrate 10 Things! What Showed Up?

What Energy can I Be Today?

34:

Question

Ask

WWIT?

Today I'd like help with:

Questfirmation

Affirm

Why? How?

Questfirmations: Why? How?

Clear

Activate

De-Story, Transform Release

Any Thoughts, Feelings, Images Coming Up?

Celebrate

Appreciate

Woohooo!!

Celebrate 10 Things! What Showed Up?

What Energy can I Be Today?

35:

Today I'd like help with:

Ask

WWIT?

Questfirmation

Questfirmations: Why? How?

Affirm

Why? How?

Clear

Any Thoughts, Feelings, Images Coming Up?

Activate

De-Story, Transform
Release

Celebrate

Celebrate 10 Things! What Showed Up?

Appreciate

Woohooo!!

What Energy can I Be Today?

36:

Question

Ask

WWIT?

Today I'd like help with:

Questfirmation

Affirm

Why? How?

Questfirmations: Why? How?

Clear

Activate

De-Story, Transform Release

Any Thoughts, Feelings, Images Coming Up?

Celebrate

Appreciate

Woohooo!!

Celebrate 10 Things! What Showed Up?

What Energy can I Be Today?

37:

Question | Today I'd like help with:

Ask
WWIT?

Questfirmation | Questfirmations: Why? How?

Affirm
Why? How?

Clear | Any Thoughts, Feelings, Images Coming Up?

Activate
De-Story, Transform
Release

Celebrate | Celebrate 10 Things! What Showed Up?

Appreciate
Woohooo!!

What Energy can I Be Today?

38:

Question

Ask
WWIT?

Today I'd like help with:

Questfirmation

Affirm
Why? How?

Questfirmations: Why? How?

Clear

Activate
De-Story, Transform
Release

Any Thoughts, Feelings, Images Coming Up?

Celebrate

Appreciate
Woohooo!!

Celebrate 10 Things! What Showed Up?

What Energy can I Be Today?

39:

Question

Ask

WWIT?

Today I'd like help with:

Questfirmation

Affirm

Why? How?

Questfirmations: Why? How?

Clear

Activate

**De-Story, Transform
Release**

Any Thoughts, Feelings, Images Coming Up?

Celebrate

Appreciate

Woohooo!!

Celebrate 10 Things! What Showed Up?

What Energy can I Be Today?

40:

Question

Ask

WWIT?

Today I'd like help with:

Questfirmation

Affirm

Why? How?

Questfirmations: Why? How?

Clear

Activate

De-Story, Transform Release

Any Thoughts, Feelings, Images Coming Up?

Celebrate

Appreciate

Woohooo!!

Celebrate 10 Things! What Showed Up?

What Energy can I Be Today?

41:

Ask

WWIT?

Today I'd like help with:

Questfirmation

Affirm

Why? How?

Questfirmations: Why? How?

Clear

Activate

De-Story, Transform Release

Any Thoughts, Feelings, Images Coming Up?

Celebrate

Appreciate

Woohooo!!

Celebrate 10 Things! What Showed Up?

What Energy can I Be Today?

42:

Question

Ask
WWIT?

Today I'd like help with:

Questfirmation

Affirm
Why? How?

Questfirmations: Why? How?

Clear

Activate
De-Story, Transform Release

Any Thoughts, Feelings, Images Coming Up?

Celebrate

Appreciate
Woohooo!!

Celebrate 10 Things! What Showed Up?

What Energy can I Be Today?

43:

Question

Ask

WWIT?

Today I'd like help with:

Questfirmation

Affirm

Why? How?

Questfirmations: Why? How?

Clear

Activate

De-Story, Transform Release

Any Thoughts, Feelings, Images Coming Up?

Celebrate

Appreciate

Woohooo!!

Celebrate 10 Things! What Showed Up?

What Energy can I Be Today?

44:

Question
Ask
WWIT?

Today I'd like help with:

Questfirmation
Affirm
Why? How?

Questfirmations: Why? How?

Clear
Activate
De-Story, Transform Release

Any Thoughts, Feelings, Images Coming Up?

Celebrate
Appreciate
Woohooo!!

Celebrate 10 Things! What Showed Up?

What Energy can I Be Today?

45:

Question

Ask

WWIT?

Today I'd like help with:

Questfirmation

Affirm

Why? How?

Questfirmations: Why? How?

Clear

Activate

De-Story, Transform
Release

Any Thoughts, Feelings, Images Coming Up?

Celebrate

Appreciate

Woohooo!!

Celebrate 10 Things! What Showed Up?

What Energy can I Be Today?

46:

Question

Ask

WWIT?

Today I'd like help with:

Questfirmation

Affirm

Why? How?

Questfirmations: Why? How?

Clear

Activate

De-Story, Transform Release

Any Thoughts, Feelings, Images Coming Up?

Celebrate

Appreciate

Woohooo!!

Celebrate 10 Things! What Showed Up?

What Energy can I Be Today?

47:

Question

Ask

WWIT?

Today I'd like help with:

Questfirmation

Affirm

Why? How?

Questfirmations: Why? How?

Clear

Activate

De-Story, Transform Release

Any Thoughts, Feelings, Images Coming Up?

Celebrate

Appreciate

Woohooo!!

Celebrate 10 Things! What Showed Up?

What Energy can I Be Today?

48:

Question

Ask

WWIT?

Today I'd like help with:

Questfirmation

Affirm

Why? How?

Questfirmations: Why? How?

Clear

Activate

De-Story, Transform Release

Any Thoughts, Feelings, Images Coming Up?

Celebrate

Appreciate

Woohooo!!

Celebrate 10 Things! What Showed Up?

What Energy can I Be Today?

49:

Question

Ask

WWIT?

Today I'd like help with:

Questfirmation

Affirm

Why? How?

Questfirmations: Why? How?

Clear

Activate

De-Story, Transform Release

Any Thoughts, Feelings, Images Coming Up?

Celebrate

Appreciate

Woohooo!!

Celebrate 10 Things! What Showed Up?

What Energy can I Be Today?

50:

Question

Ask

WWIT?

Today I'd like help with:

Questfirmation

Affirm

Why? How?

Questfirmations: Why? How?

Clear

Activate

De-Story, Transform Release

Any Thoughts, Feelings, Images Coming Up?

Celebrate

Appreciate

Woohooo!!

Celebrate 10 Things! What Showed Up?

What Energy can I Be Today?

51:

Question

Ask

WWIT?

Today I'd like help with:

Questfirmation

Affirm

Why? How?

Questfirmations: Why? How?

Clear

Activate

De-Story, Transform Release

Any Thoughts, Feelings, Images Coming Up?

Celebrate

Appreciate

Woohooo!!

Celebrate 10 Things! What Showed Up?

What Energy can I Be Today?

52:

Question

Ask

WWIT?

Today I'd like help with:

Questfirmation

Affirm

Why? How?

Questfirmations: Why? How?

Clear

Activate

De-Story, Transform Release

Any Thoughts, Feelings, Images Coming Up?

Celebrate

Appreciate

Woohooo!!

Celebrate 10 Things! What Showed Up?

What Energy can I Be Today?

53:

Question

Ask

WWIT?

Today I'd like help with:

Questfirmation

Affirm

Why? How?

Questfirmations: Why? How?

Clear

Activate

De-Story, Transform Release

Any Thoughts, Feelings, Images Coming Up?

Celebrate

Appreciate

Woohooo!!

Celebrate 10 Things! What Showed Up?

What Energy can I Be Today?

54:

Question

Ask

WWIT?

Today I'd like help with:

Questfirmation

Affirm

Why? How?

Questfirmations: Why? How?

Clear

Activate

De-Story, Transform Release

Any Thoughts, Feelings, Images Coming Up?

Celebrate

Appreciate

Woohooo!!

Celebrate 10 Things! What Showed Up?

What Energy can I Be Today?

55:

Question

Ask

WWIT?

Today I'd like help with:

Questfirmation

Affirm

Why? How?

Questfirmations: Why? How?

Clear

Activate

De-Story, Transform Release

Any Thoughts, Feelings, Images Coming Up?

Celebrate

Appreciate

Woohooo!!

Celebrate 10 Things! What Showed Up?

What Energy can I Be Today?

56:

Question

Ask

WWIT?

Today I'd like help with:

Questfirmation

Affirm

Why? How?

Questfirmations: Why? How?

Clear

Activate

De-Story, Transform Release

Any Thoughts, Feelings, Images Coming Up?

Celebrate

Appreciate

Woohooo!!

Celebrate 10 Things! What Showed Up?

What Energy can I Be Today?

57:

Today I'd like help with:

Ask

WWIT?

Questfirmation

Questfirmations: Why? How?

Affirm

Why? How?

Clear

Any Thoughts, Feelings, Images Coming Up?

Activate

De-Story, Transform Release

Celebrate

Celebrate 10 Things! What Showed Up?

Appreciate

Woohooo!!

What Energy can I Be Today?

58:

Question

Ask

WWIT?

Today I'd like help with:

Questfirmation

Affirm

Why? How?

Questfirmations: Why? How?

Clear

Activate

De-Story, Transform Release

Any Thoughts, Feelings, Images Coming Up?

Celebrate

Appreciate

Woohooo!!

Celebrate 10 Things! What Showed Up?

What Energy can I Be Today?

59:

Ask

WWIT?

Today I'd like help with:

Questfirmation

Affirm

Why? How?

Questfirmations: Why? How?

Clear

Activate

De-Story, Transform Release

Any Thoughts, Feelings, Images Coming Up?

Celebrate

Appreciate

Woohooo!!

Celebrate 10 Things! What Showed Up?

What Energy can I Be Today?

60:

Question

Ask

WWIT?

Today I'd like help with:

Questfirmation

Affirm

Why? How?

Questfirmations: Why? How?

Clear

Activate

De-Story, Transform Release

Any Thoughts, Feelings, Images Coming Up?

Celebrate

Appreciate

Woohooo!!

Celebrate 10 Things! What Showed Up?

What Energy can I Be Today?

Appreciate How Far You've Come!!

Woohoooo!! You're 30 days in - what's changed? Review your Overall Goals - are you noticing changes yet? Do your goals need to be updated?

What, if anything, needs to be changed or added to your process? Write down your thoughts here.

61:

Question

Ask
WWIT?

Today I'd like help with:

Questfirmation

Affirm
Why? How?

Questfirmations: Why? How?

Clear

Activate
De-Story, Transform Release

Any Thoughts, Feelings, Images Coming Up?

Celebrate

Appreciate
Woohooo!!

Celebrate 10 Things! What Showed Up?

What Energy can I Be Today?

62:

Question

Ask

WWIT?

Today I'd like help with:

Questfirmation

Affirm

Why? How?

Questfirmations: Why? How?

Clear

Activate

De-Story, Transform Release

Any Thoughts, Feelings, Images Coming Up?

Celebrate

Appreciate

Woohooo!!

Celebrate 10 Things! What Showed Up?

What Energy can I Be Today?

63:

Ask

WWIT?

Today I'd like help with:

Questfirmation

Affirm

Why? How?

Questfirmations: Why? How?

Clear

Activate

**De-Story, Transform
Release**

Any Thoughts, Feelings, Images Coming Up?

Celebrate

Appreciate

Woohooo!!

Celebrate 10 Things! What Showed Up?

What Energy can I Be Today?

64:

Question

Today I'd like help with:

Ask

WWIT?

Questfirmation

Questfirmations: Why? How?

Affirm

Why? How?

Clear

Any Thoughts, Feelings, Images Coming Up?

Activate

De-Story, Transform Release

Celebrate

Celebrate 10 Things! What Showed Up?

Appreciate

Woohooo!!

What Energy can I Be Today?

65:

Question

Ask

WWIT?

Today I'd like help with:

Questfirmation

Affirm

Why? How?

Questfirmations: Why? How?

Clear

Activate

De-Story, Transform Release

Any Thoughts, Feelings, Images Coming Up?

Celebrate

Appreciate

Woohooo!!

Celebrate 10 Things! What Showed Up?

What Energy can I Be Today?

66:

Question

Ask

WWIT?

Today I'd like help with:

Questfirmation

Affirm

Why? How?

Questfirmations: Why? How?

Clear

Activate

De-Story, Transform Release

Any Thoughts, Feelings, Images Coming Up?

Celebrate

Appreciate

Woohooo!!

Celebrate 10 Things! What Showed Up?

What Energy can I Be Today?

67:

Ask

WWIT?

Today I'd like help with:

Questfirmation

Affirm

Why? How?

Questfirmations: Why? How?

Clear

Activate

De-Story, Transform Release

Any Thoughts, Feelings, Images Coming Up?

Celebrate

Appreciate

Woohooo!!

Celebrate 10 Things! What Showed Up?

What Energy can I Be Today?

68:

Question

Ask

WWIT?

Today I'd like help with:

Questfirmation

Affirm

Why? How?

Questfirmations: Why? How?

Clear

Activate

De-Story, Transform Release

Any Thoughts, Feelings, Images Coming Up?

Celebrate

Appreciate

Woohooo!!

Celebrate 10 Things! What Showed Up?

What Energy can I Be Today?

69:

Question

Ask

WWIT?

Today I'd like help with:

Questfirmation

Affirm

Why? How?

Questfirmations: Why? How?

Clear

Activate

De-Story, Transform Release

Any Thoughts, Feelings, Images Coming Up?

Celebrate

Appreciate

Woohooo!!

Celebrate 10 Things! What Showed Up?

What Energy can I Be Today?

70:

Question

Ask
WWIT?

Today I'd like help with:

Questfirmation

Affirm
Why? How?

Questfirmations: Why? How?

Clear

Activate
De-Story, Transform
Release

Any Thoughts, Feelings, Images Coming Up?

Celebrate

Appreciate
Woohooo!!

Celebrate 10 Things! What Showed Up?

What Energy can I Be Today?

71:

Question

Ask

WWIT?

Today I'd like help with:

Questfirmation

Affirm

Why? How?

Questfirmations: Why? How?

Clear

Activate

De-Story, Transform
Release

Any Thoughts, Feelings, Images Coming Up?

Celebrate

Appreciate

Woohooo!!

Celebrate 10 Things! What Showed Up?

What Energy can I Be Today?

72:

Question

Ask

WWIT?

Today I'd like help with:

Questfirmation

Affirm

Why? How?

Questfirmations: Why? How?

Clear

Activate

De-Story, Transform Release

Any Thoughts, Feelings, Images Coming Up?

Celebrate

Appreciate

Woohooo!!

Celebrate 10 Things! What Showed Up?

What Energy can I Be Today?

73:

Question

Ask

WWIT?

Today I'd like help with:

Questfirmation

Affirm

Why? How?

Questfirmations: Why? How?

Clear

Activate

De-Story, Transform Release

Any Thoughts, Feelings, Images Coming Up?

Celebrate

Appreciate

Woohooo!!

Celebrate 10 Things! What Showed Up?

What Energy can I Be Today?

74:

Question

Ask

WWIT?

Today I'd like help with:

Questfirmation

Affirm

Why? How?

Questfirmations: Why? How?

Clear

Activate

De-Story, Transform Release

Any Thoughts, Feelings, Images Coming Up?

Celebrate

Appreciate

Woohooo!!

Celebrate 10 Things! What Showed Up?

What Energy can I Be Today?

75:

Question

Ask

WWIT?

Today I'd like help with:

Questfirmation

Affirm

Why? How?

Questfirmations: Why? How?

Clear

Activate

De-Story, Transform Release

Any Thoughts, Feelings, Images Coming Up?

Celebrate

Appreciate

Woohooo!!

Celebrate 10 Things! What Showed Up?

What Energy can I Be Today?

76:

Ask

WWIT?

Today I'd like help with:

Questfirmation

Affirm

Why? How?

Questfirmations: Why? How?

Clear

Activate

De-Story, Transform Release

Any Thoughts, Feelings, Images Coming Up?

Celebrate

Appreciate

Woohooo!!

Celebrate 10 Things! What Showed Up?

What Energy can I Be Today?

77:

Question

Ask

WWIT?

Today I'd like help with:

Questfirmation

Affirm

Why? How?

Questfirmations: Why? How?

Clear

Activate

De-Story, Transform Release

Any Thoughts, Feelings, Images Coming Up?

Celebrate

Appreciate

Woohooo!!

Celebrate 10 Things! What Showed Up?

What Energy can I Be Today?

78:

Question

Ask

WWIT?

Today I'd like help with:

Questfirmation

Affirm

Why? How?

Questfirmations: Why? How?

Clear

Activate

De-Story, Transform Release

Any Thoughts, Feelings, Images Coming Up?

Celebrate

Appreciate

Woohooo!!

Celebrate 10 Things! What Showed Up?

What Energy can I Be Today?

Question

Ask

WWIT?

Today I'd like help with:

Questfirmation

Affirm

Why? How?

Questfirmations: Why? How?

Clear

Activate

De-Story, Transform Release

Any Thoughts, Feelings, Images Coming Up?

Celebrate

Appreciate

Woohooo!!

Celebrate 10 Things! What Showed Up?

What Energy can I Be Today?

80:

Question

Ask

WWIT?

Today I'd like help with:

Questfirmation

Affirm

Why? How?

Questfirmations: Why? How?

Clear

Activate

De-Story, Transform Release

Any Thoughts, Feelings, Images Coming Up?

Celebrate

Appreciate

Woohooo!!

Celebrate 10 Things! What Showed Up?

What Energy can I Be Today?

81:

Question

Ask

WWIT?

Today I'd like help with:

Questfirmation

Affirm

Why? How?

Questfirmations: Why? How?

Clear

Activate

De-Story, Transform Release

Any Thoughts, Feelings, Images Coming Up?

Celebrate

Appreciate

Woohooo!!

Celebrate 10 Things! What Showed Up?

What Energy can I Be Today?

82:

Question

Ask

WWIT?

Today I'd like help with:

Questfirmation

Affirm

Why? How?

Questfirmations: Why? How?

Clear

Activate

De-Story, Transform Release

Any Thoughts, Feelings, Images Coming Up?

Celebrate

Appreciate

Woohooo!!

Celebrate 10 Things! What Showed Up?

What Energy can I Be Today?

83:

Question

Ask

WWIT?

Today I'd like help with:

Questfirmation

Affirm

Why? How?

Questfirmations: Why? How?

Clear

Activate

De-Story, Transform Release

Any Thoughts, Feelings, Images Coming Up?

Celebrate

Appreciate

Woohooo!!

Celebrate 10 Things! What Showed Up?

What Energy can I Be Today?

84:

Question

Ask

WWIT?

Today I'd like help with:

Questfirmation

Affirm

Why? How?

Questfirmations: Why? How?

Clear

Activate

De-Story, Transform Release

Any Thoughts, Feelings, Images Coming Up?

Celebrate

Appreciate

Woohooo!!

Celebrate 10 Things! What Showed Up?

What Energy can I Be Today?

85:

Question

Ask
WWIT?

Today I'd like help with:

Questfirmation

Affirm
Why? How?

Questfirmations: Why? How?

Clear

Activate
De-Story, Transform
Release

Any Thoughts, Feelings, Images Coming Up?

Celebrate

Appreciate
Woohooo!!

Celebrate 10 Things! What Showed Up?

What Energy can I Be Today?

86:

Question

Ask

WWIT?

Today I'd like help with:

Questfirmation

Affirm

Why? How?

Questfirmations: Why? How?

Clear

Activate

De-Story, Transform Release

Any Thoughts, Feelings, Images Coming Up?

Celebrate

Appreciate

Woohooo!!

Celebrate 10 Things! What Showed Up?

What Energy can I Be Today?

87:

Question

Ask

WWIT?

Today I'd like help with:

Questfirmation

Affirm

Why? How?

Questfirmations: Why? How?

Clear

Activate

De-Story, Transform Release

Any Thoughts, Feelings, Images Coming Up?

Celebrate

Appreciate

Woohooo!!

Celebrate 10 Things! What Showed Up?

What Energy can I Be Today?

88:

Question

Ask

WWIT?

Today I'd like help with:

Questfirmation

Affirm

Why? How?

Questfirmations: Why? How?

Clear

Activate

De-Story, Transform
Release

Any Thoughts, Feelings, Images Coming Up?

Celebrate

Appreciate

Woohooo!!

Celebrate 10 Things! What Showed Up?

What Energy can I Be Today?

89:

Question

Ask

WWIT?

Today I'd like help with:

Questfirmation

Affirm

Why? How?

Questfirmations: Why? How?

Clear

Activate

De-Story, Transform Release

Any Thoughts, Feelings, Images Coming Up?

Celebrate

Appreciate

Woohooo!!

Celebrate 10 Things! What Showed Up?

What Energy can I Be Today?

90:

Question

Ask

WWIT?

Today I'd like help with:

Questfirmation

Affirm

Why? How?

Questfirmations: Why? How?

Clear

Activate

De-Story, Transform Release

Any Thoughts, Feelings, Images Coming Up?

Celebrate

Appreciate

Woohooo!!

Celebrate 10 Things! What Showed Up?

What Energy can I Be Today?

You Are 90 days in - What has Changed

Take a good, honest look - I bet you've accomplished way more
than you think you have. Acknowledge that here!

91:

Question

Ask

WWIT?

Today I'd like help with:

Questfirmation

Affirm

Why? How?

Questfirmations: Why? How?

Clear

Activate

De-Story, Transform
Release

Any Thoughts, Feelings, Images Coming Up?

Celebrate

Appreciate

Woohooo!!

Celebrate 10 Things! What Showed Up?

What Energy can I Be Today?

92:

Question

Ask

WWIT?

Today I'd like help with:

Questfirmation

Affirm

Why? How?

Questfirmations: Why? How?

Clear

Activate

De-Story, Transform Release

Any Thoughts, Feelings, Images Coming Up?

Celebrate

Appreciate

Woohooo!!

Celebrate 10 Things! What Showed Up?

What Energy can I Be Today?

93:

Today I'd like help with:

Ask

WWIT?

Questfirmation

Questfirmations: Why? How?

Affirm

Why? How?

Clear

Any Thoughts, Feelings, Images Coming Up?

Activate

De-Story, Transform
Release

Celebrate

Celebrate 10 Things! What Showed Up?

Appreciate

Woohooo!!

What Energy can I Be Today?

94:

Question

Ask
WWIT?

Today I'd like help with:

Questfirmation

Affirm
Why? How?

Questfirmations: Why? How?

Clear

Activate
De-Story, Transform Release

Any Thoughts, Feelings, Images Coming Up?

Celebrate

Appreciate
Woohooo!!

Celebrate 10 Things! What Showed Up?

What Energy can I Be Today?

95:

Question

Ask

WWIT?

Today I'd like help with:

Questfirmation

Affirm

Why? How?

Questfirmations: Why? How?

Clear

Activate

De-Story, Transform Release

Any Thoughts, Feelings, Images Coming Up?

Celebrate

Appreciate

Woohooo!!

Celebrate 10 Things! What Showed Up?

What Energy can I Be Today?

96:

Question

Ask

WWIT?

Today I'd like help with:

Questfirmation

Affirm

Why? How?

Questfirmations: Why? How?

Clear

Activate

De-Story, Transform Release

Any Thoughts, Feelings, Images Coming Up?

Celebrate

Appreciate

Woohooo!!

Celebrate 10 Things! What Showed Up?

What Energy can I Be Today?

97:

Question

Ask

WWIT?

Today I'd like help with:

Questfirmation

Affirm

Why? How?

Questfirmations: Why? How?

Clear

Activate

De-Story, Transform Release

Any Thoughts, Feelings, Images Coming Up?

Celebrate

Appreciate

Woohooo!!

Celebrate 10 Things! What Showed Up?

What Energy can I Be Today?

98:

Question

Ask

WWIT?

Today I'd like help with:

Questfirmation

Affirm

Why? How?

Questfirmations: Why? How?

Clear

Activate

De-Story, Transform Release

Any Thoughts, Feelings, Images Coming Up?

Celebrate

Appreciate

Woohooo!!

Celebrate 10 Things! What Showed Up?

What Energy can I Be Today?

99:

Question

Ask

WWIT?

Today I'd like help with:

Questfirmation

Affirm

Why? How?

Questfirmations: Why? How?

Clear

Activate

De-Story, Transform Release

Any Thoughts, Feelings, Images Coming Up?

Celebrate

Appreciate

Woohooo!!

Celebrate 10 Things! What Showed Up?

What Energy can I Be Today?

100:

Question

Ask

WWIT?

Today I'd like help with:

Questfirmation

Affirm

Why? How?

Questfirmations: Why? How?

Clear

Activate

De-Story, Transform Release

Any Thoughts, Feelings, Images Coming Up?

Celebrate

Appreciate

Woohooo!!

Celebrate 10 Things! What Showed Up?

What Energy can I Be Today?

101:

Question

Ask

WWIT?

Today I'd like help with:

Questfirmation

Affirm

Why? How?

Questfirmations: Why? How?

Clear

Activate

De-Story, Transform
Release

Any Thoughts, Feelings, Images Coming Up?

Celebrate

Appreciate

Woohooo!!

Celebrate 10 Things! What Showed Up?

What Energy can I Be Today?

102:

Question

Ask

WWIT?

Today I'd like help with:

Questfirmation

Affirm

Why? How?

Questfirmations: Why? How?

Clear

Activate

De-Story, Transform Release

Any Thoughts, Feelings, Images Coming Up?

Celebrate

Appreciate

Woohooo!!

Celebrate 10 Things! What Showed Up?

What Energy can I Be Today?

103:

Question

Ask
WWIT?

Today I'd like help with:

Questfirmation

Affirm
Why? How?

Questfirmations: Why? How?

Clear

Activate
De-Story, Transform
Release

Any Thoughts, Feelings, Images Coming Up?

Celebrate

Appreciate
Woohooo!!

Celebrate 10 Things! What Showed Up?

What Energy can I Be Today?

104:

Question

Ask

WWIT?

Today I'd like help with:

Questfirmation

Affirm

Why? How?

Questfirmations: Why? How?

Clear

Activate

De-Story, Transform Release

Any Thoughts, Feelings, Images Coming Up?

Celebrate

Appreciate

Woohooo!!

Celebrate 10 Things! What Showed Up?

What Energy can I Be Today?

105:

Question

Ask
WWIT?

Today I'd like help with:

Questfirmation

Affirm
Why? How?

Questfirmations: Why? How?

Clear

Activate
De-Story, Transform
Release

Any Thoughts, Feelings, Images Coming Up?

Celebrate

Appreciate
Woohooo!!

Celebrate 10 Things! What Showed Up?

What Energy can I Be Today?

106:

Question

Ask
WWIT?

Today I'd like help with:

Questfirmation

Affirm
Why? How?

Questfirmations: Why? How?

Clear

Activate
De-Story, Transform
Release

Any Thoughts, Feelings, Images Coming Up?

Celebrate

Appreciate
Woohooo!!

Celebrate 10 Things! What Showed Up?

What Energy can I Be Today?

107:

Question

Ask

WWIT?

Today I'd like help with:

Questfirmation

Affirm

Why? How?

Questfirmations: Why? How?

Clear

Activate

De-Story, Transform Release

Any Thoughts, Feelings, Images Coming Up?

Celebrate

Appreciate

Woohooo!!

Celebrate 10 Things! What Showed Up?

What Energy can I Be Today?

108:

Question

Ask

WWIT?

Today I'd like help with:

Questfirmation

Affirm

Why? How?

Questfirmations: Why? How?

Clear

Activate

De-Story, Transform Release

Any Thoughts, Feelings, Images Coming Up?

Celebrate

Appreciate

Woohooo!!

Celebrate 10 Things! What Showed Up?

What Energy can I Be Today?

109:

Question

Ask

WWIT?

Today I'd like help with:

Questfirmation

Affirm

Why? How?

Questfirmations: Why? How?

Clear

Activate

De-Story, Transform
Release

Any Thoughts, Feelings, Images Coming Up?

Celebrate

Appreciate

Woohooo!!

Celebrate 10 Things! What Showed Up?

What Energy can I Be Today?

110:

Question

Ask

WWIT?

Today I'd like help with:

Questfirmation

Affirm

Why? How?

Questfirmations: Why? How?

Clear

Activate

De-Story, Transform Release

Any Thoughts, Feelings, Images Coming Up?

Celebrate

Appreciate

Woohooo!!

Celebrate 10 Things! What Showed Up?

What Energy can I Be Today?

111:

Question

Ask

WWIT?

Today I'd like help with:

Questfirmation

Affirm

Why? How?

Questfirmations: Why? How?

Clear

Activate

De-Story, Transform Release

Any Thoughts, Feelings, Images Coming Up?

Celebrate

Appreciate

Woohooo!!

Celebrate 10 Things! What Showed Up?

What Energy can I Be Today?

112:

Question

Ask

WWIT?

Today I'd like help with:

Questfirmation

Affirm

Why? How?

Questfirmations: Why? How?

Clear

Activate

De-Story, Transform Release

Any Thoughts, Feelings, Images Coming Up?

Celebrate

Appreciate

Woohooo!!

Celebrate 10 Things! What Showed Up?

What Energy can I Be Today?

113:

Question

Ask

WWIT?

Today I'd like help with:

Questfirmation

Affirm

Why? How?

Questfirmations: Why? How?

Clear

Activate

De-Story, Transform Release

Any Thoughts, Feelings, Images Coming Up?

Celebrate

Appreciate

Woohooo!!

Celebrate 10 Things! What Showed Up?

What Energy can I Be Today?

114:

Question

Ask

WWIT?

Today I'd like help with:

Questfirmation

Affirm

Why? How?

Questfirmations: Why? How?

Clear

Activate

De-Story, Transform Release

Any Thoughts, Feelings, Images Coming Up?

Celebrate

Appreciate

Woohooo!!

Celebrate 10 Things! What Showed Up?

What Energy can I Be Today?

115:

Today I'd like help with:

Ask
WWIT?

Questfirmation
Questfirmations: Why? How?

Affirm
Why? How?

Clear
Any Thoughts, Feelings, Images Coming Up?

Activate
De-Story, Transform Release

Celebrate
Celebrate 10 Things! What Showed Up?

Appreciate
Woohooo!!

What Energy can I Be Today?

116:

Question

Ask

WWIT?

Today I'd like help with:

Questfirmation

Affirm

Why? How?

Questfirmations: Why? How?

Clear

Activate

De-Story, Transform Release

Any Thoughts, Feelings, Images Coming Up?

Celebrate

Appreciate

Woohooo!!

Celebrate 10 Things! What Showed Up?

What Energy can I Be Today?

117:

Question

Ask

WWIT?

Today I'd like help with:

Questfirmation

Affirm

Why? How?

Questfirmations: Why? How?

Clear

Activate

De-Story, Transform Release

Any Thoughts, Feelings, Images Coming Up?

Celebrate

Appreciate

Woohooo!!

Celebrate 10 Things! What Showed Up?

What Energy can I Be Today?

118:

Question

Ask

WWIT?

Today I'd like help with:

Questfirmation

Affirm

Why? How?

Questfirmations: Why? How?

Clear

Activate

**De-Story, Transform
Release**

Any Thoughts, Feelings, Images Coming Up?

Celebrate

Appreciate

Woohooo!!

Celebrate 10 Things! What Showed Up?

What Energy can I Be Today?

119:

Question Today I'd like help with:

Ask

WWIT?

Questfirmation Questfirmations: Why? How?

Affirm

Why? How?

Clear Any Thoughts, Feelings, Images Coming Up?

Activate

De-Story, Transform Release

Celebrate Celebrate 10 Things! What Showed Up?

Appreciate

Woohooo!!

What Energy can I Be Today?

120:

Question

Ask

WWIT?

Today I'd like help with:

Questfirmation

Affirm

Why? How?

Questfirmations: Why? How?

Clear

Activate

De-Story, Transform
Release

Any Thoughts, Feelings, Images Coming Up?

Celebrate

Appreciate

Woohooo!!

Celebrate 10 Things! What Showed Up?

What Energy can I Be Today?

120 days in - Woohooo!!

Seriously, who does this? Who sticks with a program this long? I'll tell you, only successful people!   Again, this is a good time to acknowledge what has shown up and trust that what hasn't, is on it's way.

Keep clearing.

*Remember, you don't need to do this alone - check out the different programs I have available to get help if you want it - go to **AttractMoreNow.com.***

121:

Question

Ask

WWIT?

Today I'd like help with:

Questfirmation

Affirm

Why? How?

Questfirmations: Why? How?

Clear

Activate

De-Story, Transform Release

Any Thoughts, Feelings, Images Coming Up?

Celebrate

Appreciate

Woohooo!!

Celebrate 10 Things! What Showed Up?

What Energy can I Be Today?

122:

Question

Ask

WWIT?

Today I'd like help with:

Questfirmation

Affirm

Why? How?

Questfirmations: Why? How?

Clear

Activate

De-Story, Transform Release

Any Thoughts, Feelings, Images Coming Up?

Celebrate

Appreciate

Woohooo!!

Celebrate 10 Things! What Showed Up?

What Energy can I Be Today?

123:

Today I'd like help with:

Ask

WWIT?

Questfirmation

Questfirmations: Why? How?

Affirm

Why? How?

Clear

Any Thoughts, Feelings, Images Coming Up?

Activate

De-Story, Transform Release

Celebrate

Celebrate 10 Things! What Showed Up?

Appreciate

Woohooo!!

What Energy can I Be Today?

124:

Question

Ask

WWIT?

Today I'd like help with:

Questfirmation

Affirm

Why? How?

Questfirmations: Why? How?

Clear

Activate

De-Story, Transform Release

Any Thoughts, Feelings, Images Coming Up?

Celebrate

Appreciate

Woohooo!!

Celebrate 10 Things! What Showed Up?

What Energy can I Be Today?

125:

Question

Ask

WWIT?

Today I'd like help with:

Questfirmation

Affirm

Why? How?

Questfirmations: Why? How?

Clear

Activate

De-Story, Transform Release

Any Thoughts, Feelings, Images Coming Up?

Celebrate

Appreciate

Woohooo!!

Celebrate 10 Things! What Showed Up?

What Energy can I Be Today?

126:

Ask
WWIT?

Today I'd like help with:

Questfirmation

Affirm
Why? How?

Questfirmations: Why? How?

Clear

Activate
De-Story, Transform
Release

Any Thoughts, Feelings, Images Coming Up?

Celebrate

Appreciate
Woohooo!!

Celebrate 10 Things! What Showed Up?

What Energy can I Be Today?

127:

Question

Ask

WWIT?

Today I'd like help with:

Questfirmation

Affirm

Why? How?

Questfirmations: Why? How?

Clear

Activate

De-Story, Transform Release

Any Thoughts, Feelings, Images Coming Up?

Celebrate

Appreciate

Woohooo!!

Celebrate 10 Things! What Showed Up?

What Energy can I Be Today?

128:

Question

Ask
WWIT?

Today I'd like help with:

Questfirmation

Affirm
Why? How?

Questfirmations: Why? How?

Clear

Activate
De-Story, Transform Release

Any Thoughts, Feelings, Images Coming Up?

Celebrate

Appreciate
Woohooo!!

Celebrate 10 Things! What Showed Up?

What Energy can I Be Today?

129:

Question

Ask

WWIT?

Today I'd like help with:

Questfirmation

Affirm

Why? How?

Questfirmations: Why? How?

Clear

Activate

De-Story, Transform
Release

Any Thoughts, Feelings, Images Coming Up?

Celebrate

Appreciate

Woohooo!!

Celebrate 10 Things! What Showed Up?

What Energy can I Be Today?

130:

Ask

WWIT?

Today I'd like help with:

Questfirmation

Affirm

Why? How?

Questfirmations: Why? How?

Clear

Activate

De-Story, Transform Release

Any Thoughts, Feelings, Images Coming Up?

Celebrate

Appreciate

Woohooo!!

Celebrate 10 Things! What Showed Up?

What Energy can I Be Today?

131:

Question

Ask

WWIT?

Today I'd like help with:

Questfirmation

Affirm

Why? How?

Questfirmations: Why? How?

Clear

Activate

De-Story, Transform Release

Any Thoughts, Feelings, Images Coming Up?

Celebrate

Appreciate

Woohooo!!

Celebrate 10 Things! What Showed Up?

What Energy can I Be Today?

132:

Question

Ask

WWIT?

Today I'd like help with:

Questfirmation

Affirm

Why? How?

Questfirmations: Why? How?

Clear

Activate

De-Story, Transform Release

Any Thoughts, Feelings, Images Coming Up?

Celebrate

Appreciate

Woohooo!!

Celebrate 10 Things! What Showed Up?

What Energy can I Be Today?

133:

Question

Ask

WWIT?

Today I'd like help with:

Questfirmation

Affirm

Why? How?

Questfirmations: Why? How?

Clear

Activate

De-Story, Transform
Release

Any Thoughts, Feelings, Images Coming Up?

Celebrate

Appreciate

Woohooo!!

Celebrate 10 Things! What Showed Up?

What Energy can I Be Today?

134:

Question

Ask

WWIT?

Today I'd like help with:

Questfirmation

Affirm

Why? How?

Questfirmations: Why? How?

Clear

Activate

De-Story, Transform Release

Any Thoughts, Feelings, Images Coming Up?

Celebrate

Appreciate

Woohooo!!

Celebrate 10 Things! What Showed Up?

What Energy can I Be Today?

135:

Question

Ask

WWIT?

Today I'd like help with:

Questfirmation

Affirm

Why? How?

Questfirmations: Why? How?

Clear

Activate

De-Story, Transform Release

Any Thoughts, Feelings, Images Coming Up?

Celebrate

Appreciate

Woohooo!!

Celebrate 10 Things! What Showed Up?

What Energy can I Be Today?

136:

Question

Ask
WWIT?

Today I'd like help with:

Questfirmation

Affirm
Why? How?

Questfirmations: Why? How?

Clear

Activate
De-Story, Transform
Release

Any Thoughts, Feelings, Images Coming Up?

Celebrate

Appreciate
Woohooo!!

Celebrate 10 Things! What Showed Up?

What Energy can I Be Today?

137:

Question

Ask

WWIT?

Today I'd like help with:

Questfirmation

Affirm

Why? How?

Questfirmations: Why? How?

Clear

Activate

De-Story, Transform Release

Any Thoughts, Feelings, Images Coming Up?

Celebrate

Appreciate

Woohooo!!

Celebrate 10 Things! What Showed Up?

What Energy can I Be Today?

138:

Question

Ask

WWIT?

Today I'd like help with:

Questfirmation

Affirm

Why? How?

Questfirmations: Why? How?

Clear

Activate

De-Story, Transform Release

Any Thoughts, Feelings, Images Coming Up?

Celebrate

Appreciate

Woohooo!!

Celebrate 10 Things! What Showed Up?

What Energy can I Be Today?

139:

Question

Ask

WWIT?

Today I'd like help with:

Questfirmation

Affirm

Why? How?

Questfirmations: Why? How?

Clear

Activate

De-Story, Transform Release

Any Thoughts, Feelings, Images Coming Up?

Celebrate

Appreciate

Woohooo!!

Celebrate 10 Things! What Showed Up?

What Energy can I Be Today?

140:

Question

Ask

WWIT?

Today I'd like help with:

Questfirmation

Affirm

Why? How?

Questfirmations: Why? How?

Clear

Activate

De-Story, Transform Release

Any Thoughts, Feelings, Images Coming Up?

Celebrate

Appreciate

Woohooo!!

Celebrate 10 Things! What Showed Up?

What Energy can I Be Today?

141:

Question

Ask

WWIT?

Today I'd like help with:

Questfirmation

Affirm

Why? How?

Questfirmations: Why? How?

Clear

Activate

De-Story, Transform
Release

Any Thoughts, Feelings, Images Coming Up?

Celebrate

Appreciate

Woohooo!!

Celebrate 10 Things! What Showed Up?

What Energy can I Be Today?

142:

Question

Ask

WWIT?

Today I'd like help with:

Questfirmation

Affirm

Why? How?

Questfirmations: Why? How?

Clear

Activate

De-Story, Transform Release

Any Thoughts, Feelings, Images Coming Up?

Celebrate

Appreciate

Woohooo!!

Celebrate 10 Things! What Showed Up?

What Energy can I Be Today?

143:

Question

Ask

WWIT?

Today I'd like help with:

Questfirmation

Affirm

Why? How?

Questfirmations: Why? How?

Clear

Activate

De-Story, Transform Release

Any Thoughts, Feelings, Images Coming Up?

Celebrate

Appreciate

Woohooo!!

Celebrate 10 Things! What Showed Up?

What Energy can I Be Today?

144:

Question

Ask
WWIT?

Today I'd like help with:

Questfirmation

Affirm
Why? How?

Questfirmations: Why? How?

Clear

Activate
De-Story, Transform Release

Any Thoughts, Feelings, Images Coming Up?

Celebrate

Appreciate
Woohooo!!

Celebrate 10 Things! What Showed Up?

What Energy can I Be Today?

145:

Question

Today I'd like help with:

Ask
WWIT?

Questfirmation

Questfirmations: Why? How?

Affirm
Why? How?

Clear

Any Thoughts, Feelings, Images Coming Up?

Activate
De-Story, Transform
Release

Celebrate

Celebrate 10 Things! What Showed Up?

Appreciate
Woohooo!!

What Energy can I Be Today?

146:

Question

Ask
WWIT?

Today I'd like help with:

Questfirmation

Affirm
Why? How?

Questfirmations: Why? How?

Clear

Activate
De-Story, Transform
Release

Any Thoughts, Feelings, Images Coming Up?

Celebrate

Appreciate
Woohooo!!

Celebrate 10 Things! What Showed Up?

What Energy can I Be Today?

147:

Question

Ask

WWIT?

Today I'd like help with:

Questfirmation

Affirm

Why? How?

Questfirmations: Why? How?

Clear

Activate

De-Story, Transform Release

Any Thoughts, Feelings, Images Coming Up?

Celebrate

Appreciate

Woohooo!!

Celebrate 10 Things! What Showed Up?

What Energy can I Be Today?

148:

Ask
WWIT?

Today I'd like help with:

Affirm
Why? How?

Questfirmations: Why? How?

Activate
De-Story, Transform Release

Any Thoughts, Feelings, Images Coming Up?

Appreciate
Woohooo!!

Celebrate 10 Things! What Showed Up?

What Energy can I Be Today?

149:

Ask

WWIT?

Today I'd like help with:

Questfirmation

Affirm

Why? How?

Questfirmations: Why? How?

Clear

Activate

De-Story, Transform
Release

Any Thoughts, Feelings, Images Coming Up?

Celebrate

Appreciate

Woohooo!!

Celebrate 10 Things! What Showed Up?

What Energy can I Be Today?

150:

Ask

WWIT?

Today I'd like help with:

Questfirmation

Affirm

Why? How?

Questfirmations: Why? How?

Clear

Activate

De-Story, Transform
Release

Any Thoughts, Feelings, Images Coming Up?

Celebrate

Appreciate

Woohooo!!

Celebrate 10 Things! What Showed Up?

What Energy can I Be Today?

151:

Question

Ask

WWIT?

Today I'd like help with:

Questfirmation

Affirm

Why? How?

Questfirmations: Why? How?

Clear

Activate

De-Story, Transform
Release

Any Thoughts, Feelings, Images Coming Up?

Celebrate

Appreciate

Woohooo!!

Celebrate 10 Things! What Showed Up?

What Energy can I Be Today?

152:

Question

Ask

WWIT?

Today I'd like help with:

Questfirmation

Affirm

Why? How?

Questfirmations: Why? How?

Clear

Activate

De-Story, Transform Release

Any Thoughts, Feelings, Images Coming Up?

Celebrate

Appreciate

Woohooo!!

Celebrate 10 Things! What Showed Up?

What Energy can I Be Today?

153:

Question

Ask

WWIT?

Today I'd like help with:

Questfirmation

Affirm

Why? How?

Questfirmations: Why? How?

Clear

Activate

De-Story, Transform Release

Any Thoughts, Feelings, Images Coming Up?

Celebrate

Appreciate

Woohooo!!

Celebrate 10 Things! What Showed Up?

What Energy can I Be Today?

154:

Question

Ask

WWIT?

Today I'd like help with:

Questfirmation

Affirm

Why? How?

Questfirmations: Why? How?

Clear

Activate

De-Story, Transform Release

Any Thoughts, Feelings, Images Coming Up?

Celebrate

Appreciate

Woohooo!!

Celebrate 10 Things! What Showed Up?

What Energy can I Be Today?

155:

Question

Ask

WWIT?

Today I'd like help with:

Questfirmation

Affirm

Why? How?

Questfirmations: Why? How?

Clear

Activate

De-Story, Transform Release

Any Thoughts, Feelings, Images Coming Up?

Celebrate

Appreciate

Woohooo!!

Celebrate 10 Things! What Showed Up?

What Energy can I Be Today?

156:

Question

Ask

WWIT?

Today I'd like help with:

Questfirmation

Affirm

Why? How?

Questfirmations: Why? How?

Clear

Activate

De-Story, Transform Release

Any Thoughts, Feelings, Images Coming Up?

Celebrate

Appreciate

Woohooo!!

Celebrate 10 Things! What Showed Up?

What Energy can I Be Today?

157:

Question

Ask

WWIT?

Today I'd like help with:

Questfirmation

Affirm

Why? How?

Questfirmations: Why? How?

Clear

Activate

De-Story, Transform
Release

Any Thoughts, Feelings, Images Coming Up?

Celebrate

Appreciate

Woohooo!!

Celebrate 10 Things! What Showed Up?

What Energy can I Be Today?

158:

Today I'd like help with:

Ask

WWIT?

Questfirmation

Questfirmations: Why? How?

Affirm

Why? How?

Clear

Any Thoughts, Feelings, Images Coming Up?

Activate

De-Story, Transform Release

Celebrate

Celebrate 10 Things! What Showed Up?

Appreciate

Woohooo!!

What Energy can I Be Today?

159:

Question

Ask

WWIT?

Today I'd like help with:

Questfirmation

Affirm

Why? How?

Questfirmations: Why? How?

Clear

Activate

De-Story, Transform
Release

Any Thoughts, Feelings, Images Coming Up?

Celebrate

Appreciate

Woohooo!!

Celebrate 10 Things! What Showed Up?

What Energy can I Be Today?

160:

Question

Ask

WWIT?

Today I'd like help with:

Questfirmation

Affirm

Why? How?

Questfirmations: Why? How?

Clear

Activate

De-Story, Transform Release

Any Thoughts, Feelings, Images Coming Up?

Celebrate

Appreciate

Woohooo!!

Celebrate 10 Things! What Showed Up?

What Energy can I Be Today?

161:

Question

Ask
WWIT?

Today I'd like help with:

Questfirmation

Affirm
Why? How?

Questfirmations: Why? How?

Clear

Activate
**De-Story, Transform
Release**

Any Thoughts, Feelings, Images Coming Up?

Celebrate

Appreciate
Woohooo!!

Celebrate 10 Things! What Showed Up?

What Energy can I Be Today?

162:

Question

Ask
WWIT?

Today I'd like help with:

Questfirmation

Affirm
Why? How?

Questfirmations: Why? How?

Clear

Activate
De-Story, Transform
Release

Any Thoughts, Feelings, Images Coming Up?

Celebrate

Appreciate
Woohooo!!

Celebrate 10 Things! What Showed Up?

What Energy can I Be Today?

163:

Question

Ask

WWIT?

Today I'd like help with:

Questfirmation

Affirm

Why? How?

Questfirmations: Why? How?

Clear

Activate

De-Story, Transform
Release

Any Thoughts, Feelings, Images Coming Up?

Celebrate

Appreciate

Woohooo!!

Celebrate 10 Things! What Showed Up?

What Energy can I Be Today?

164:

Question

Ask

WWIT?

Today I'd like help with:

Questfirmation

Affirm

Why? How?

Questfirmations: Why? How?

Clear

Activate

De-Story, Transform Release

Any Thoughts, Feelings, Images Coming Up?

Celebrate

Appreciate

Woohooo!!

Celebrate 10 Things! What Showed Up?

What Energy can I Be Today?

165:

Today I'd like help with:

Ask

WWIT?

Questfirmation

Questfirmations: Why? How?

Affirm

Why? How?

Clear

Any Thoughts, Feelings, Images Coming Up?

Activate

De-Story, Transform Release

Celebrate

Celebrate 10 Things! What Showed Up?

Appreciate

Woohooo!!

What Energy can I Be Today?

166:

Question

Ask

WWIT?

Today I'd like help with:

Questfirmation

Affirm

Why? How?

Questfirmations: Why? How?

Clear

Activate

De-Story, Transform Release

Any Thoughts, Feelings, Images Coming Up?

Celebrate

Appreciate

Woohooo!!

Celebrate 10 Things! What Showed Up?

What Energy can I Be Today?

167:

Question

Ask

WWIT?

Today I'd like help with:

Questfirmation

Affirm

Why? How?

Questfirmations: Why? How?

Clear

Activate

De-Story, Transform Release

Any Thoughts, Feelings, Images Coming Up?

Celebrate

Appreciate

Woohooo!!

Celebrate 10 Things! What Showed Up?

What Energy can I Be Today?

168:

Question

Ask

WWIT?

Today I'd like help with:

Questfirmation

Affirm

Why? How?

Questfirmations: Why? How?

Clear

Activate

De-Story, Transform Release

Any Thoughts, Feelings, Images Coming Up?

Celebrate

Appreciate

Woohooo!!

Celebrate 10 Things! What Showed Up?

What Energy can I Be Today?

169:

Question

Ask

WWIT?

Today I'd like help with:

Questfirmation

Affirm

Why? How?

Questfirmations: Why? How?

Clear

Activate

De-Story, Transform
Release

Any Thoughts, Feelings, Images Coming Up?

Celebrate

Appreciate

Woohooo!!

Celebrate 10 Things! What Showed Up?

What Energy can I Be Today?

170:

Question

Ask

WWIT?

Today I'd like help with:

Questfirmation

Affirm

Why? How?

Questfirmations: Why? How?

Clear

Activate

De-Story, Transform
Release

Any Thoughts, Feelings, Images Coming Up?

Celebrate

Appreciate

Woohooo!!

Celebrate 10 Things! What Showed Up?

What Energy can I Be Today?

171:

Question

Ask

WWIT?

Today I'd like help with:

Questfirmation

Affirm

Why? How?

Questfirmations: Why? How?

Clear

Activate

De-Story, Transform
Release

Any Thoughts, Feelings, Images Coming Up?

Celebrate

Appreciate

Woohooo!!

Celebrate 10 Things! What Showed Up?

What Energy can I Be Today?

172:

Question

Ask
WWIT?

Today I'd like help with:

Questfirmation

Affirm
Why? How?

Questfirmations: Why? How?

Clear

Activate
De-Story, Transform Release

Any Thoughts, Feelings, Images Coming Up?

Celebrate

Appreciate
Woohooo!!

Celebrate 10 Things! What Showed Up?

What Energy can I Be Today?

173:

Question
Ask
WWIT?

Today I'd like help with:

Questfirmation
Affirm
Why? How?

Questfirmations: Why? How?

Clear
Activate
De-Story, Transform Release

Any Thoughts, Feelings, Images Coming Up?

Celebrate
Appreciate
Woohooo!!

Celebrate 10 Things! What Showed Up?

What Energy can I Be Today?

174:

Question

Ask

WWIT?

Today I'd like help with:

Questfirmation

Affirm

Why? How?

Questfirmations: Why? How?

Clear

Activate

De-Story, Transform Release

Any Thoughts, Feelings, Images Coming Up?

Celebrate

Appreciate

Woohooo!!

Celebrate 10 Things! What Showed Up?

What Energy can I Be Today?

175:

Question

Ask

WWIT?

Today I'd like help with:

Questfirmation

Affirm

Why? How?

Questfirmations: Why? How?

Clear

Activate

De-Story, Transform
Release

Any Thoughts, Feelings, Images Coming Up?

Celebrate

Appreciate

Woohooo!!

Celebrate 10 Things! What Showed Up?

What Energy can I Be Today?

176:

Question
Ask
WWIT?

Today I'd like help with:

Questfirmation
Affirm
Why? How?

Questfirmations: Why? How?

Clear
Activate
De-Story, Transform Release

Any Thoughts, Feelings, Images Coming Up?

Celebrate
Appreciate
Woohooo!!

Celebrate 10 Things! What Showed Up?

What Energy can I Be Today?

177:

Question

Ask

WWIT?

Today I'd like help with:

Questfirmation

Affirm

Why? How?

Questfirmations: Why? How?

Clear

Activate

De-Story, Transform
Release

Any Thoughts, Feelings, Images Coming Up?

Celebrate

Appreciate

Woohooo!!

Celebrate 10 Things! What Showed Up?

What Energy can I Be Today?

178:

Question

Ask

WWIT?

Today I'd like help with:

Questfirmation

Affirm

Why? How?

Questfirmations: Why? How?

Clear

Activate

De-Story, Transform Release

Any Thoughts, Feelings, Images Coming Up?

Celebrate

Appreciate

Woohooo!!

Celebrate 10 Things! What Showed Up?

What Energy can I Be Today?

179:

Question

Ask

WWIT?

Today I'd like help with:

Questfirmation

Affirm

Why? How?

Questfirmations: Why? How?

Clear

Activate

De-Story, Transform Release

Any Thoughts, Feelings, Images Coming Up?

Celebrate

Appreciate

Woohooo!!

Celebrate 10 Things! What Showed Up?

What Energy can I Be Today?

180:

Question

Ask

WWIT?

Today I'd like help with:

Questfirmation

Affirm

Why? How?

Questfirmations: Why? How?

Clear

Activate

De-Story, Transform Release

Any Thoughts, Feelings, Images Coming Up?

Celebrate

Appreciate

Woohooo!!

Celebrate 10 Things! What Showed Up?

What Energy can I Be Today?

Six Months!!

Wow!! How amazing are you?!! You know the drill, now's a good time to review and update!!

181:

Question

Ask

WWIT?

Today I'd like help with:

Questfirmation

Affirm

Why? How?

Questfirmations: Why? How?

Clear

Activate

De-Story, Transform
Release

Any Thoughts, Feelings, Images Coming Up?

Celebrate

Appreciate

Woohooo!!

Celebrate 10 Things! What Showed Up?

What Energy can I Be Today?

182:

Question

Ask

WWIT?

Today I'd like help with:

Questfirmation

Affirm

Why? How?

Questfirmations: Why? How?

Clear

Activate

De-Story, Transform
Release

Any Thoughts, Feelings, Images Coming Up?

Celebrate

Appreciate

Woohooo!!

Celebrate 10 Things! What Showed Up?

What Energy can I Be Today?

183:

Question

Ask

WWIT?

Today I'd like help with:

Questfirmation

Affirm

Why? How?

Questfirmations: Why? How?

Clear

Activate

De-Story, Transform Release

Any Thoughts, Feelings, Images Coming Up?

Celebrate

Appreciate

Woohooo!!

Celebrate 10 Things! What Showed Up?

What Energy can I Be Today?

184:

Question

Ask
WWIT?

Today I'd like help with:

Questfirmation

Affirm
Why? How?

Questfirmations: Why? How?

Clear

Activate
De-Story, Transform Release

Any Thoughts, Feelings, Images Coming Up?

Celebrate

Appreciate
Woohooo!!

Celebrate 10 Things! What Showed Up?

What Energy can I Be Today?

185:

Question

Ask

WWIT?

Today I'd like help with:

Questfirmation

Affirm

Why? How?

Questfirmations: Why? How?

Clear

Activate

De-Story, Transform
Release

Any Thoughts, Feelings, Images Coming Up?

Celebrate

Appreciate

Woohooo!!

Celebrate 10 Things! What Showed Up?

What Energy can I Be Today?

186:

Question
Ask
WWIT?

Today I'd like help with:

Questfirmation
Affirm
Why? How?

Questfirmations: Why? How?

Clear
Activate
De-Story, Transform Release

Any Thoughts, Feelings, Images Coming Up?

Celebrate
Appreciate
Woohooo!!

Celebrate 10 Things! What Showed Up?

What Energy can I Be Today?

187:

Question

Ask
WWIT?

Today I'd like help with:

Questfirmation

Affirm
Why? How?

Questfirmations: Why? How?

Clear

Activate
De-Story, Transform
Release

Any Thoughts, Feelings, Images Coming Up?

Celebrate

Appreciate
Woohooo!!

Celebrate 10 Things! What Showed Up?

What Energy can I Be Today?

188:

Question

Ask
WWIT?

Today I'd like help with:

Questfirmation

Affirm
Why? How?

Questfirmations: Why? How?

Clear

Activate
De-Story, Transform
Release

Any Thoughts, Feelings, Images Coming Up?

Celebrate

Appreciate
Woohooo!!

Celebrate 10 Things! What Showed Up?

What Energy can I Be Today?

189:

Question

Ask

WWIT?

Today I'd like help with:

Questfirmation

Affirm

Why? How?

Questfirmations: Why? How?

Clear

Activate

De-Story, Transform Release

Any Thoughts, Feelings, Images Coming Up?

Celebrate

Appreciate

Woohooo!!

Celebrate 10 Things! What Showed Up?

What Energy can I Be Today?

190:

Question

Ask

WWIT?

Today I'd like help with:

Questfirmation

Affirm

Why? How?

Questfirmations: Why? How?

Clear

Activate

De-Story, Transform Release

Any Thoughts, Feelings, Images Coming Up?

Celebrate

Appreciate

Woohooo!!

Celebrate 10 Things! What Showed Up?

What Energy can I Be Today?

191:

Question

Ask
WWIT?

Today I'd like help with:

Questfirmation

Affirm
Why? How?

Questfirmations: Why? How?

Clear

Activate
De-Story, Transform
Release

Any Thoughts, Feelings, Images Coming Up?

Celebrate

Appreciate
Woohooo!!

Celebrate 10 Things! What Showed Up?

What Energy can I Be Today?

192:

Question

Ask

WWIT?

Today I'd like help with:

Questfirmation

Affirm

Why? How?

Questfirmations: Why? How?

Clear

Activate

De-Story, Transform Release

Any Thoughts, Feelings, Images Coming Up?

Celebrate

Appreciate

Woohooo!!

Celebrate 10 Things! What Showed Up?

What Energy can I Be Today?

193:

Question

Ask

WWIT?

Today I'd like help with:

Questfirmation

Affirm

Why? How?

Questfirmations: Why? How?

Clear

Activate

De-Story, Transform Release

Any Thoughts, Feelings, Images Coming Up?

Celebrate

Appreciate

Woohooo!!

Celebrate 10 Things! What Showed Up?

What Energy can I Be Today?

194:

Question

Ask

WWIT?

Today I'd like help with:

Questfirmation

Affirm

Why? How?

Questfirmations: Why? How?

Clear

Activate

De-Story, Transform Release

Any Thoughts, Feelings, Images Coming Up?

Celebrate

Appreciate

Woohooo!!

Celebrate 10 Things! What Showed Up?

What Energy can I Be Today?

195:

Today I'd like help with:

Ask

WWIT?

Questfirmation

Questfirmations: Why? How?

Affirm

Why? How?

Clear

Any Thoughts, Feelings, Images Coming Up?

Activate

De-Story, Transform Release

Celebrate

Celebrate 10 Things! What Showed Up?

Appreciate

Woohooo!!

What Energy can I Be Today?

196:

Question

Ask

WWIT?

Today I'd like help with:

Questfirmation

Affirm

Why? How?

Questfirmations: Why? How?

Clear

Activate

De-Story, Transform Release

Any Thoughts, Feelings, Images Coming Up?

Celebrate

Appreciate

Woohooo!!

Celebrate 10 Things! What Showed Up?

What Energy can I Be Today?

197:

Question — Today I'd like help with:

Ask
WWIT?

Questfirmation — Questfirmations: Why? How?

Affirm
Why? How?

Clear — Any Thoughts, Feelings, Images Coming Up?

Activate
De-Story, Transform Release

Celebrate — Celebrate 10 Things! What Showed Up?

Appreciate
Woohooo!!

What Energy can I Be Today?

198:

Question

Ask

WWIT?

Today I'd like help with:

Questfirmation

Affirm

Why? How?

Questfirmations: Why? How?

Clear

Activate

De-Story, Transform Release

Any Thoughts, Feelings, Images Coming Up?

Celebrate

Appreciate

Woohooo!!

Celebrate 10 Things! What Showed Up?

What Energy can I Be Today?

199:

Question

Ask

WWIT?

Today I'd like help with:

Questfirmation

Affirm

Why? How?

Questfirmations: Why? How?

Clear

Activate

De-Story, Transform Release

Any Thoughts, Feelings, Images Coming Up?

Celebrate

Appreciate

Woohooo!!

Celebrate 10 Things! What Showed Up?

What Energy can I Be Today?

200:

Question

Ask
WWIT?

Today I'd like help with:

Questfirmation

Affirm
Why? How?

Questfirmations: Why? How?

Clear

Activate
De-Story, Transform Release

Any Thoughts, Feelings, Images Coming Up?

Celebrate

Appreciate
Woohooo!!

Celebrate 10 Things! What Showed Up?

What Energy can I Be Today?

201:

Question

Ask

WWIT?

Today I'd like help with:

Questfirmation

Affirm

Why? How?

Questfirmations: Why? How?

Clear

Activate

De-Story, Transform Release

Any Thoughts, Feelings, Images Coming Up?

Celebrate

Appreciate

Woohooo!!

Celebrate 10 Things! What Showed Up?

What Energy can I Be Today?

202:

Question

Ask
WWIT?

Today I'd like help with:

Questfirmation

Affirm
Why? How?

Questfirmations: Why? How?

Clear

Activate
De-Story, Transform Release

Any Thoughts, Feelings, Images Coming Up?

Celebrate

Appreciate
Woohooo!!

Celebrate 10 Things! What Showed Up?

What Energy can I Be Today?

203:

Question

Ask

WWIT?

Today I'd like help with:

Questfirmation

Affirm

Why? How?

Questfirmations: Why? How?

Clear

Activate

De-Story, Transform Release

Any Thoughts, Feelings, Images Coming Up?

Celebrate

Appreciate

Woohooo!!

Celebrate 10 Things! What Showed Up?

What Energy can I Be Today?

204:

Question

Ask
WWIT?

Today I'd like help with:

Questfirmation

Affirm
Why? How?

Questfirmations: Why? How?

Clear

Activate
De-Story, Transform Release

Any Thoughts, Feelings, Images Coming Up?

Celebrate

Appreciate
Woohooo!!

Celebrate 10 Things! What Showed Up?

What Energy can I Be Today?

205:

Question

Ask
WWIT?

Today I'd like help with:

Questfirmation

Affirm
Why? How?

Questfirmations: Why? How?

Clear

Activate
De-Story, Transform
Release

Any Thoughts, Feelings, Images Coming Up?

Celebrate

Appreciate
Woohooo!!

Celebrate 10 Things! What Showed Up?

What Energy can I Be Today?

206:

Question

Ask

WWIT?

Today I'd like help with:

Questfirmation

Affirm

Why? How?

Questfirmations: Why? How?

Clear

Activate

De-Story, Transform Release

Any Thoughts, Feelings, Images Coming Up?

Celebrate

Appreciate

Woohooo!!

Celebrate 10 Things! What Showed Up?

What Energy can I Be Today?

207:

Question

Ask
WWIT?

Today I'd like help with:

Questfirmation

Affirm
Why? How?

Questfirmations: Why? How?

Clear

Activate
De-Story, Transform Release

Any Thoughts, Feelings, Images Coming Up?

Celebrate

Appreciate
Woohooo!!

Celebrate 10 Things! What Showed Up?

What Energy can I Be Today?

208:

Question

Ask
WWIT?

Today I'd like help with:

Questfirmation

Affirm
Why? How?

Questfirmations: Why? How?

Clear

Activate
De-Story, Transform
Release

Any Thoughts, Feelings, Images Coming Up?

Celebrate

Appreciate
Woohooo!!

Celebrate 10 Things! What Showed Up?

What Energy can I Be Today?

209:

Today I'd like help with:

Ask
WWIT?

Questfirmation

Questfirmations: Why? How?

Affirm
Why? How?

Clear

Any Thoughts, Feelings, Images Coming Up?

Activate
De-Story, Transform
Release

Celebrate

Celebrate 10 Things! What Showed Up?

Appreciate
Woohooo!!

What Energy can I Be Today?

210:

Question

Ask
WWIT?

Today I'd like help with:

Questfirmation

Affirm
Why? How?

Questfirmations: Why? How?

Clear

Activate
De-Story, Transform Release

Any Thoughts, Feelings, Images Coming Up?

Celebrate

Appreciate
Woohooo!!

Celebrate 10 Things! What Showed Up?

What Energy can I Be Today?

211:

Question

Ask
WWIT?

Today I'd like help with:

Questfirmation

Affirm
Why? How?

Questfirmations: Why? How?

Clear

Activate
De-Story, Transform
Release

Any Thoughts, Feelings, Images Coming Up?

Celebrate

Appreciate
Woohooo!!

Celebrate 10 Things! What Showed Up?

What Energy can I Be Today?

212:

Question

Ask
WWIT?

Today I'd like help with:

Questfirmation

Affirm
Why? How?

Questfirmations: Why? How?

Clear

Activate
De-Story, Transform Release

Any Thoughts, Feelings, Images Coming Up?

Celebrate

Appreciate
Woohooo!!

Celebrate 10 Things! What Showed Up?

What Energy can I Be Today?

213:

Question

Ask

WWIT?

Today I'd like help with:

Questfirmation

Affirm

Why? How?

Questfirmations: Why? How?

Clear

Activate

De-Story, Transform Release

Any Thoughts, Feelings, Images Coming Up?

Celebrate

Appreciate

Woohooo!!

Celebrate 10 Things! What Showed Up?

What Energy can I Be Today?

214:

Question

Ask

WWIT?

Today I'd like help with:

Questfirmation

Affirm

Why? How?

Questfirmations: Why? How?

Clear

Activate

De-Story, Transform Release

Any Thoughts, Feelings, Images Coming Up?

Celebrate

Appreciate

Woohooo!!

Celebrate 10 Things! What Showed Up?

What Energy can I Be Today?

215:

Question

Ask

WWIT?

Today I'd like help with:

Questfirmation

Affirm

Why? How?

Questfirmations: Why? How?

Clear

Activate

De-Story, Transform Release

Any Thoughts, Feelings, Images Coming Up?

Celebrate

Appreciate

Woohooo!!

Celebrate 10 Things! What Showed Up?

What Energy can I Be Today?

216:

Ask

WWIT?

Today I'd like help with:

Questfirmation

Affirm

Why? How?

Questfirmations: Why? How?

Clear

Activate

De-Story, Transform Release

Any Thoughts, Feelings, Images Coming Up?

Celebrate

Appreciate

Woohooo!!

Celebrate 10 Things! What Showed Up?

What Energy can I Be Today?

217:

Question

Ask

WWIT?

Today I'd like help with:

Questfirmation

Affirm

Why? How?

Questfirmations: Why? How?

Clear

Activate

De-Story, Transform Release

Any Thoughts, Feelings, Images Coming Up?

Celebrate

Appreciate

Woohooo!!

Celebrate 10 Things! What Showed Up?

What Energy can I Be Today?

218:

Question

Ask

WWIT?

Today I'd like help with:

Questfirmation

Affirm

Why? How?

Questfirmations: Why? How?

Clear

Activate

De-Story, Transform Release

Any Thoughts, Feelings, Images Coming Up?

Celebrate

Appreciate

Woohooo!!

Celebrate 10 Things! What Showed Up?

What Energy can I Be Today?

219:

Today I'd like help with:

Ask

WWIT?

Questfirmation

Questfirmations: Why? How?

Affirm

Why? How?

Clear

Any Thoughts, Feelings, Images Coming Up?

Activate

De-Story, Transform
Release

Celebrate

Celebrate 10 Things! What Showed Up?

Appreciate

Woohooo!!

What Energy can I Be Today?

220:

Question

Ask

WWIT?

Today I'd like help with:

Questfirmation

Affirm

Why? How?

Questfirmations: Why? How?

Clear

Activate

De-Story, Transform Release

Any Thoughts, Feelings, Images Coming Up?

Celebrate

Appreciate

Woohooo!!

Celebrate 10 Things! What Showed Up?

What Energy can I Be Today?

221:

Question

Ask
WWIT?

Today I'd like help with:

Questfirmation

Affirm
Why? How?

Questfirmations: Why? How?

Clear

Activate
De-Story, Transform Release

Any Thoughts, Feelings, Images Coming Up?

Celebrate

Appreciate
Woohooo!!

Celebrate 10 Things! What Showed Up?

What Energy can I Be Today?

222:

Question

Ask
WWIT?

Today I'd like help with:

Questfirmation

Affirm
Why? How?

Questfirmations: Why? How?

Clear

Activate
De-Story, Transform Release

Any Thoughts, Feelings, Images Coming Up?

Celebrate

Appreciate
Woohooo!!

Celebrate 10 Things! What Showed Up?

What Energy can I Be Today?

223:

Question

Ask
WWIT?

Today I'd like help with:

Questfirmation

Affirm
Why? How?

Questfirmations: Why? How?

Clear

Activate
De-Story, Transform
Release

Any Thoughts, Feelings, Images Coming Up?

Celebrate

Appreciate
Woohooo!!

Celebrate 10 Things! What Showed Up?

What Energy can I Be Today?

224:

Question

Ask

WWIT?

Today I'd like help with:

Questfirmation

Affirm

Why? How?

Questfirmations: Why? How?

Clear

Activate

De-Story, Transform Release

Any Thoughts, Feelings, Images Coming Up?

Celebrate

Appreciate

Woohooo!!

Celebrate 10 Things! What Showed Up?

What Energy can I Be Today?

225:

Question

Ask

WWIT?

Today I'd like help with:

Questfirmation

Affirm

Why? How?

Questfirmations: Why? How?

Clear

Activate

De-Story, Transform Release

Any Thoughts, Feelings, Images Coming Up?

Celebrate

Appreciate

Woohooo!!

Celebrate 10 Things! What Showed Up?

What Energy can I Be Today?

226:

Question

Ask

WWIT?

Today I'd like help with:

Questfirmation

Affirm

Why? How?

Questfirmations: Why? How?

Clear

Activate

De-Story, Transform Release

Any Thoughts, Feelings, Images Coming Up?

Celebrate

Appreciate

Woohooo!!

Celebrate 10 Things! What Showed Up?

What Energy can I Be Today?

227:

Question

Ask

WWIT?

Today I'd like help with:

Questfirmation

Affirm

Why? How?

Questfirmations: Why? How?

Clear

Activate

De-Story, Transform Release

Any Thoughts, Feelings, Images Coming Up?

Celebrate

Appreciate

Woohooo!!

Celebrate 10 Things! What Showed Up?

What Energy can I Be Today?

228:

Question

Ask
WWIT?

Today I'd like help with:

Questfirmation

Affirm
Why? How?

Questfirmations: Why? How?

Clear

Activate
**De-Story, Transform
Release**

Any Thoughts, Feelings, Images Coming Up?

Celebrate

Appreciate
Woohooo!!

Celebrate 10 Things! What Showed Up?

What Energy can I Be Today?

229:

Question

Ask

WWIT?

Today I'd like help with:

Questfirmation

Affirm

Why? How?

Questfirmations: Why? How?

Clear

Activate

De-Story, Transform Release

Any Thoughts, Feelings, Images Coming Up?

Celebrate

Appreciate

Woohooo!!

Celebrate 10 Things! What Showed Up?

What Energy can I Be Today?

230:

Question

Ask

WWIT?

Today I'd like help with:

Questfirmation

Affirm

Why? How?

Questfirmations: Why? How?

Clear

Activate

De-Story, Transform Release

Any Thoughts, Feelings, Images Coming Up?

Celebrate

Appreciate

Woohooo!!

Celebrate 10 Things! What Showed Up?

What Energy can I Be Today?

231:

Question

Ask

WWIT?

Today I'd like help with:

Questfirmation

Affirm

Why? How?

Questfirmations: Why? How?

Clear

Activate

De-Story, Transform Release

Any Thoughts, Feelings, Images Coming Up?

Celebrate

Appreciate

Woohooo!!

Celebrate 10 Things! What Showed Up?

What Energy can I Be Today?

232:

Question

Ask

WWIT?

Today I'd like help with:

Questfirmation

Affirm

Why? How?

Questfirmations: Why? How?

Clear

Activate

De-Story, Transform Release

Any Thoughts, Feelings, Images Coming Up?

Celebrate

Appreciate

Woohooo!!

Celebrate 10 Things! What Showed Up?

What Energy can I Be Today?

233:

Question

Ask

WWIT?

Today I'd like help with:

Questfirmation

Affirm

Why? How?

Questfirmations: Why? How?

Clear

Activate

De-Story, Transform Release

Any Thoughts, Feelings, Images Coming Up?

Celebrate

Appreciate

Woohooo!!

Celebrate 10 Things! What Showed Up?

What Energy can I Be Today?

234:

Question

Ask

WWIT?

Today I'd like help with:

Questfirmation

Affirm

Why? How?

Questfirmations: Why? How?

Clear

Activate

De-Story, Transform Release

Any Thoughts, Feelings, Images Coming Up?

Celebrate

Appreciate

Woohooo!!

Celebrate 10 Things! What Showed Up?

What Energy can I Be Today?

235:

Question

Ask

WWIT?

Today I'd like help with:

Questfirmation

Affirm

Why? How?

Questfirmations: Why? How?

Clear

Activate

De-Story, Transform Release

Any Thoughts, Feelings, Images Coming Up?

Celebrate

Appreciate

Woohooo!!

Celebrate 10 Things! What Showed Up?

What Energy can I Be Today?

236:

Question

Ask

WWIT?

Today I'd like help with:

Questfirmation

Affirm

Why? How?

Questfirmations: Why? How?

Clear

Activate

De-Story, Transform Release

Any Thoughts, Feelings, Images Coming Up?

Celebrate

Appreciate

Woohooo!!

Celebrate 10 Things! What Showed Up?

What Energy can I Be Today?

237:

Question

Ask

WWIT?

Today I'd like help with:

Questfirmation

Affirm

Why? How?

Questfirmations: Why? How?

Clear

Activate

De-Story, Transform Release

Any Thoughts, Feelings, Images Coming Up?

Celebrate

Appreciate

Woohooo!!

Celebrate 10 Things! What Showed Up?

What Energy can I Be Today?

238:

Question

Ask
WWIT?

Today I'd like help with:

Questfirmation

Affirm
Why? How?

Questfirmations: Why? How?

Clear

Activate
De-Story, Transform Release

Any Thoughts, Feelings, Images Coming Up?

Celebrate

Appreciate
Woohooo!!

Celebrate 10 Things! What Showed Up?

What Energy can I Be Today?

239:

Question

Ask
WWIT?

Today I'd like help with:

Questfirmation

Affirm
Why? How?

Questfirmations: Why? How?

Clear

Activate
De-Story, Transform Release

Any Thoughts, Feelings, Images Coming Up?

Celebrate

Appreciate
Woohooo!!

Celebrate 10 Things! What Showed Up?

What Energy can I Be Today?

240:

Question

Ask
WWIT?

Today I'd like help with:

Questfirmation

Affirm
Why? How?

Questfirmations: Why? How?

Clear

Activate
De-Story, Transform Release

Any Thoughts, Feelings, Images Coming Up?

Celebrate

Appreciate
Woohooo!!

Celebrate 10 Things! What Showed Up?

What Energy can I Be Today?

241:

Question

Ask

WWIT?

Today I'd like help with:

Questfirmation

Affirm

Why? How?

Questfirmations: Why? How?

Clear

Activate

De-Story, Transform Release

Any Thoughts, Feelings, Images Coming Up?

Celebrate

Appreciate

Woohooo!!

Celebrate 10 Things! What Showed Up?

What Energy can I Be Today?

242:

Question

Ask

WWIT?

Today I'd like help with:

Questfirmation

Affirm

Why? How?

Questfirmations: Why? How?

Clear

Activate

De-Story, Transform Release

Any Thoughts, Feelings, Images Coming Up?

Celebrate

Appreciate

Woohooo!!

Celebrate 10 Things! What Showed Up?

What Energy can I Be Today?

243:

Question

Ask

WWIT?

Today I'd like help with:

Questfirmation

Affirm

Why? How?

Questfirmations: Why? How?

Clear

Activate

De-Story, Transform
Release

Any Thoughts, Feelings, Images Coming Up?

Celebrate

Appreciate

Woohooo!!

Celebrate 10 Things! What Showed Up?

What Energy can I Be Today?

244:

Question

Ask

WWIT?

Today I'd like help with:

Questfirmation

Affirm

Why? How?

Questfirmations: Why? How?

Clear

Activate

De-Story, Transform Release

Any Thoughts, Feelings, Images Coming Up?

Celebrate

Appreciate

Woohooo!!

Celebrate 10 Things! What Showed Up?

What Energy can I Be Today?

245:

Question

Ask

WWIT?

Today I'd like help with:

Questfirmation

Affirm

Why? How?

Questfirmations: Why? How?

Clear

Activate

De-Story, Transform Release

Any Thoughts, Feelings, Images Coming Up?

Celebrate

Appreciate

Woohooo!!

Celebrate 10 Things! What Showed Up?

What Energy can I Be Today?

246:

Question

Ask

WWIT?

Today I'd like help with:

Questfirmation

Affirm

Why? How?

Questfirmations: Why? How?

Clear

Activate

De-Story, Transform Release

Any Thoughts, Feelings, Images Coming Up?

Celebrate

Appreciate

Woohooo!!

Celebrate 10 Things! What Showed Up?

What Energy can I Be Today?

247:

Question

Ask

WWIT?

Today I'd like help with:

Questfirmation

Affirm

Why? How?

Questfirmations: Why? How?

Clear

Activate

De-Story, Transform Release

Any Thoughts, Feelings, Images Coming Up?

Celebrate

Appreciate

Woohooo!!

Celebrate 10 Things! What Showed Up?

What Energy can I Be Today?

248:

Question

Ask

WWIT?

Today I'd like help with:

Questfirmation

Affirm

Why? How?

Questfirmations: Why? How?

Clear

Activate

De-Story, Transform Release

Any Thoughts, Feelings, Images Coming Up?

Celebrate

Appreciate

Woohooo!!

Celebrate 10 Things! What Showed Up?

What Energy can I Be Today?

249:

Question

Ask

WWIT?

Today I'd like help with:

Questfirmation

Affirm

Why? How?

Questfirmations: Why? How?

Clear

Activate

De-Story, Transform
Release

Any Thoughts, Feelings, Images Coming Up?

Celebrate

Appreciate

Woohooo!!

Celebrate 10 Things! What Showed Up?

What Energy can I Be Today?

250:

Question

Ask

WWIT?

Today I'd like help with:

Questfirmation

Affirm

Why? How?

Questfirmations: Why? How?

Clear

Activate

**De-Story, Transform
Release**

Any Thoughts, Feelings, Images Coming Up?

Celebrate

Appreciate

Woohooo!!

Celebrate 10 Things! What Showed Up?

What Energy can I Be Today?

251:

Question

Ask

WWIT?

Today I'd like help with:

Questfirmation

Affirm

Why? How?

Questfirmations: Why? How?

Clear

Activate

De-Story, Transform Release

Any Thoughts, Feelings, Images Coming Up?

Celebrate

Appreciate

Woohooo!!

Celebrate 10 Things! What Showed Up?

What Energy can I Be Today?

252:

Question

Ask

WWIT?

Today I'd like help with:

Questfirmation

Affirm

Why? How?

Questfirmations: Why? How?

Clear

Activate

De-Story, Transform Release

Any Thoughts, Feelings, Images Coming Up?

Celebrate

Appreciate

Woohooo!!

Celebrate 10 Things! What Showed Up?

What Energy can I Be Today?

253:

Question

Ask
WWIT?

Today I'd like help with:

Questfirmation

Affirm
Why? How?

Questfirmations: Why? How?

Clear

Activate
De-Story, Transform Release

Any Thoughts, Feelings, Images Coming Up?

Celebrate

Appreciate
Woohooo!!

Celebrate 10 Things! What Showed Up?

What Energy can I Be Today?

254:

Question
Ask
WWIT?

Today I'd like help with:

Questfirmation
Affirm
Why? How?

Questfirmations: Why? How?

Clear
Activate
De-Story, Transform Release

Any Thoughts, Feelings, Images Coming Up?

Celebrate
Appreciate
Woohooo!!

Celebrate 10 Things! What Showed Up?

What Energy can I Be Today?

255:

Question

Ask
WWIT?

Today I'd like help with:

Questfirmation

Affirm
Why? How?

Questfirmations: Why? How?

Clear

Activate
De-Story, Transform Release

Any Thoughts, Feelings, Images Coming Up?

Celebrate

Appreciate
Woohooo!!

Celebrate 10 Things! What Showed Up?

What Energy can I Be Today?

256:

Question

Ask
WWIT?

Today I'd like help with:

Questfirmation

Affirm
Why? How?

Questfirmations: Why? How?

Clear

Activate
De-Story, Transform Release

Any Thoughts, Feelings, Images Coming Up?

Celebrate

Appreciate
Woohooo!!

Celebrate 10 Things! What Showed Up?

What Energy can I Be Today?

257:

Question

Ask

WWIT?

Today I'd like help with:

Questfirmation

Affirm

Why? How?

Questfirmations: Why? How?

Clear

Activate

De-Story, Transform Release

Any Thoughts, Feelings, Images Coming Up?

Celebrate

Appreciate

Woohooo!!

Celebrate 10 Things! What Showed Up?

What Energy can I Be Today?

258:

Question

Ask

WWIT?

Today I'd like help with:

Questfirmation

Affirm

Why? How?

Questfirmations: Why? How?

Clear

Activate

De-Story, Transform Release

Any Thoughts, Feelings, Images Coming Up?

Celebrate

Appreciate

Woohooo!!

Celebrate 10 Things! What Showed Up?

What Energy can I Be Today?

259:

Question

Ask

WWIT?

Today I'd like help with:

Questfirmation

Affirm

Why? How?

Questfirmations: Why? How?

Clear

Activate

De-Story, Transform Release

Any Thoughts, Feelings, Images Coming Up?

Celebrate

Appreciate

Woohooo!!

Celebrate 10 Things! What Showed Up?

What Energy can I Be Today?

260:

Question

Ask

WWIT?

Today I'd like help with:

Questfirmation

Affirm

Why? How?

Questfirmations: Why? How?

Clear

Activate

De-Story, Transform Release

Any Thoughts, Feelings, Images Coming Up?

Celebrate

Appreciate

Woohooo!!

Celebrate 10 Things! What Showed Up?

What Energy can I Be Today?

261:

Question

Ask
WWIT?

Today I'd like help with:

Questfirmation

Affirm
Why? How?

Questfirmations: Why? How?

Clear

Activate
De-Story, Transform Release

Any Thoughts, Feelings, Images Coming Up?

Celebrate

Appreciate
Woohooo!!

Celebrate 10 Things! What Showed Up?

What Energy can I Be Today?

262:

Question

Ask

WWIT?

Today I'd like help with:

Questfirmation

Affirm

Why? How?

Questfirmations: Why? How?

Clear

Activate

De-Story, Transform Release

Any Thoughts, Feelings, Images Coming Up?

Celebrate

Appreciate

Woohooo!!

Celebrate 10 Things! What Showed Up?

What Energy can I Be Today?

263:

Question

Ask

WWIT?

Today I'd like help with:

Questfirmation

Affirm

Why? How?

Questfirmations: Why? How?

Clear

Activate

De-Story, Transform Release

Any Thoughts, Feelings, Images Coming Up?

Celebrate

Appreciate

Woohooo!!

Celebrate 10 Things! What Showed Up?

What Energy can I Be Today?

264:

Ask
WWIT?

Today I'd like help with:

Questfirmation

Affirm
Why? How?

Questfirmations: Why? How?

Clear

Activate
De-Story, Transform
Release

Any Thoughts, Feelings, Images Coming Up?

Celebrate

Appreciate
Woohooo!!

Celebrate 10 Things! What Showed Up?

What Energy can I Be Today?

265:

Question

Ask

WWIT?

Today I'd like help with:

Questfirmation

Affirm

Why? How?

Questfirmations: Why? How?

Clear

Activate

De-Story, Transform Release

Any Thoughts, Feelings, Images Coming Up?

Celebrate

Appreciate

Woohooo!!

Celebrate 10 Things! What Showed Up?

What Energy can I Be Today?

266:

Question

Ask

WWIT?

Today I'd like help with:

Questfirmation

Affirm

Why? How?

Questfirmations: Why? How?

Clear

Activate

De-Story, Transform Release

Any Thoughts, Feelings, Images Coming Up?

Celebrate

Appreciate

Woohooo!!

Celebrate 10 Things! What Showed Up?

What Energy can I Be Today?

267:

Question

Ask

WWIT?

Today I'd like help with:

Questfirmation

Affirm

Why? How?

Questfirmations: Why? How?

Clear

Activate

De-Story, Transform Release

Any Thoughts, Feelings, Images Coming Up?

Celebrate

Appreciate

Woohooo!!

Celebrate 10 Things! What Showed Up?

What Energy can I Be Today?

268:

Question

Ask

WWIT?

Today I'd like help with:

Questfirmation

Affirm

Why? How?

Questfirmations: Why? How?

Clear

Activate

De-Story, Transform Release

Any Thoughts, Feelings, Images Coming Up?

Celebrate

Appreciate

Woohooo!!

Celebrate 10 Things! What Showed Up?

What Energy can I Be Today?

269:

Question

Ask
WWIT?

Today I'd like help with:

Questfirmation

Affirm
Why? How?

Questfirmations: Why? How?

Clear

Activate
De-Story, Transform
Release

Any Thoughts, Feelings, Images Coming Up?

Celebrate

Appreciate
Woohooo!!

Celebrate 10 Things! What Showed Up?

What Energy can I Be Today?

270:

Question

Ask
WWIT?

Today I'd like help with:

Questfirmation

Affirm
Why? How?

Questfirmations: Why? How?

Clear

Activate
De-Story, Transform
Release

Any Thoughts, Feelings, Images Coming Up?

Celebrate

Appreciate
Woohooo!!

Celebrate 10 Things! What Showed Up?

What Energy can I Be Today?

271:

Question

Ask

WWIT?

Today I'd like help with:

Questfirmation

Affirm

Why? How?

Questfirmations: Why? How?

Clear

Activate

De-Story, Transform Release

Any Thoughts, Feelings, Images Coming Up?

Celebrate

Appreciate

Woohooo!!

Celebrate 10 Things! What Showed Up?

What Energy can I Be Today?

272:

Question

Ask

WWIT?

Today I'd like help with:

Questfirmation

Affirm

Why? How?

Questfirmations: Why? How?

Clear

Activate

De-Story, Transform Release

Any Thoughts, Feelings, Images Coming Up?

Celebrate

Appreciate

Woohooo!!

Celebrate 10 Things! What Showed Up?

What Energy can I Be Today?

273:

Question

Ask

WWIT?

Today I'd like help with:

Questfirmation

Affirm

Why? How?

Questfirmations: Why? How?

Clear

Activate

De-Story, Transform Release

Any Thoughts, Feelings, Images Coming Up?

Celebrate

Appreciate

Woohooo!!

Celebrate 10 Things! What Showed Up?

What Energy can I Be Today?

274:

Question

Ask

WWIT?

Today I'd like help with:

Questfirmation

Affirm

Why? How?

Questfirmations: Why? How?

Clear

Activate

De-Story, Transform Release

Any Thoughts, Feelings, Images Coming Up?

Celebrate

Appreciate

Woohooo!!

Celebrate 10 Things! What Showed Up?

What Energy can I Be Today?

275:

Question

Ask
WWIT?

Today I'd like help with:

Questfirmation

Affirm
Why? How?

Questfirmations: Why? How?

Clear

Activate
De-Story, Transform
Release

Any Thoughts, Feelings, Images Coming Up?

Celebrate

Appreciate
Woohooo!!

Celebrate 10 Things! What Showed Up?

What Energy can I Be Today?

276:

Question

Ask

WWIT?

Today I'd like help with:

Questfirmation

Affirm

Why? How?

Questfirmations: Why? How?

Clear

Activate

De-Story, Transform Release

Any Thoughts, Feelings, Images Coming Up?

Celebrate

Appreciate

Woohooo!!

Celebrate 10 Things! What Showed Up?

What Energy can I Be Today?

277:

Question

Ask

WWIT?

Today I'd like help with:

Questfirmation

Affirm

Why? How?

Questfirmations: Why? How?

Clear

Activate

De-Story, Transform Release

Any Thoughts, Feelings, Images Coming Up?

Celebrate

Appreciate

Woohooo!!

Celebrate 10 Things! What Showed Up?

What Energy can I Be Today?

278:

Question

Ask

WWIT?

Today I'd like help with:

Questfirmation

Affirm

Why? How?

Questfirmations: Why? How?

Clear

Activate

De-Story, Transform Release

Any Thoughts, Feelings, Images Coming Up?

Celebrate

Appreciate

Woohooo!!

Celebrate 10 Things! What Showed Up?

What Energy can I Be Today?

279:

Question

Ask

WWIT?

Today I'd like help with:

Questfirmation

Affirm

Why? How?

Questfirmations: Why? How?

Clear

Activate

De-Story, Transform Release

Any Thoughts, Feelings, Images Coming Up?

Celebrate

Appreciate

Woohooo!!

Celebrate 10 Things! What Showed Up?

What Energy can I Be Today?

280:

Question

Ask

WWIT?

Today I'd like help with:

Questfirmation

Affirm

Why? How?

Questfirmations: Why? How?

Clear

Activate

De-Story, Transform Release

Any Thoughts, Feelings, Images Coming Up?

Celebrate

Appreciate

Woohooo!!

Celebrate 10 Things! What Showed Up?

What Energy can I Be Today?

281:

Question

Ask

WWIT?

Today I'd like help with:

Questfirmation

Affirm

Why? How?

Questfirmations: Why? How?

Clear

Activate

De-Story, Transform Release

Any Thoughts, Feelings, Images Coming Up?

Celebrate

Appreciate

Woohooo!!

Celebrate 10 Things! What Showed Up?

What Energy can I Be Today?

282:

Question

Ask
WWIT?

Today I'd like help with:

Questfirmation

Affirm
Why? How?

Questfirmations: Why? How?

Clear

Activate
De-Story, Transform Release

Any Thoughts, Feelings, Images Coming Up?

Celebrate

Appreciate
Woohooo!!

Celebrate 10 Things! What Showed Up?

What Energy can I Be Today?

283:

Question

Ask
WWIT?

Today I'd like help with:

Questfirmation

Affirm
Why? How?

Questfirmations: Why? How?

Clear

Activate
De-Story, Transform
Release

Any Thoughts, Feelings, Images Coming Up?

Celebrate

Appreciate
Woohooo!!

Celebrate 10 Things! What Showed Up?

What Energy can I Be Today?

284:

Question

Ask
WWIT?

Today I'd like help with:

Questfirmation

Affirm
Why? How?

Questfirmations: Why? How?

Clear

Activate
De-Story, Transform Release

Any Thoughts, Feelings, Images Coming Up?

Celebrate

Appreciate
Woohooo!!

Celebrate 10 Things! What Showed Up?

What Energy can I Be Today?

285:

Question

Ask

WWIT?

Today I'd like help with:

Questfirmation

Affirm

Why? How?

Questfirmations: Why? How?

Clear

Activate

De-Story, Transform Release

Any Thoughts, Feelings, Images Coming Up?

Celebrate

Appreciate

Woohooo!!

Celebrate 10 Things! What Showed Up?

What Energy can I Be Today?

286:

Question

Ask

WWIT?

Today I'd like help with:

Questfirmation

Affirm

Why? How?

Questfirmations: Why? How?

Clear

Activate

De-Story, Transform Release

Any Thoughts, Feelings, Images Coming Up?

Celebrate

Appreciate

Woohooo!!

Celebrate 10 Things! What Showed Up?

What Energy can I Be Today?

287:

Question

Ask

WWIT?

Today I'd like help with:

Questfirmation

Affirm

Why? How?

Questfirmations: Why? How?

Clear

Activate

De-Story, Transform Release

Any Thoughts, Feelings, Images Coming Up?

Celebrate

Appreciate

Woohooo!!

Celebrate 10 Things! What Showed Up?

What Energy can I Be Today?

288:

Question

Ask

WWIT?

Today I'd like help with:

Questfirmation

Affirm

Why? How?

Questfirmations: Why? How?

Clear

Activate

De-Story, Transform Release

Any Thoughts, Feelings, Images Coming Up?

Celebrate

Appreciate

Woohooo!!

Celebrate 10 Things! What Showed Up?

What Energy can I Be Today?

289:

Question

Ask
WWIT?

Today I'd like help with:

Questfirmation

Affirm
Why? How?

Questfirmations: Why? How?

Clear

Activate
De-Story, Transform Release

Any Thoughts, Feelings, Images Coming Up?

Celebrate

Appreciate
Woohooo!!

Celebrate 10 Things! What Showed Up?

What Energy can I Be Today?

290:

Question

Ask

WWIT?

Today I'd like help with:

Questfirmation

Affirm

Why? How?

Questfirmations: Why? How?

Clear

Activate

De-Story, Transform Release

Any Thoughts, Feelings, Images Coming Up?

Celebrate

Appreciate

Woohooo!!

Celebrate 10 Things! What Showed Up?

What Energy can I Be Today?

291:

Question

Ask

WWIT?

Today I'd like help with:

Questfirmation

Affirm

Why? How?

Questfirmations: Why? How?

Clear

Activate

De-Story, Transform Release

Any Thoughts, Feelings, Images Coming Up?

Celebrate

Appreciate

Woohooo!!

Celebrate 10 Things! What Showed Up?

What Energy can I Be Today?

292:

Question

Ask
WWIT?

Today I'd like help with:

Questfirmation

Affirm
Why? How?

Questfirmations: Why? How?

Clear

Activate
De-Story, Transform Release

Any Thoughts, Feelings, Images Coming Up?

Celebrate

Appreciate
Woohooo!!

Celebrate 10 Things! What Showed Up?

What Energy can I Be Today?

293:

Question

Ask
WWIT?

Today I'd like help with:

Questfirmation

Affirm
Why? How?

Questfirmations: Why? How?

Clear

Activate
De-Story, Transform Release

Any Thoughts, Feelings, Images Coming Up?

Celebrate

Appreciate
Woohooo!!

Celebrate 10 Things! What Showed Up?

What Energy can I Be Today?

294:

Question

Ask

WWIT?

Today I'd like help with:

Questfirmation

Affirm

Why? How?

Questfirmations: Why? How?

Clear

Activate

De-Story, Transform
Release

Any Thoughts, Feelings, Images Coming Up?

Celebrate

Appreciate

Woohooo!!

Celebrate 10 Things! What Showed Up?

What Energy can I Be Today?

295:

Question

Ask

WWIT?

Today I'd like help with:

Questfirmation

Affirm

Why? How?

Questfirmations: Why? How?

Clear

Activate

De-Story, Transform Release

Any Thoughts, Feelings, Images Coming Up?

Celebrate

Appreciate

Woohooo!!

Celebrate 10 Things! What Showed Up?

What Energy can I Be Today?

296:

Question

Ask

WWIT?

Today I'd like help with:

Questfirmation

Affirm

Why? How?

Questfirmations: Why? How?

Clear

Activate

De-Story, Transform Release

Any Thoughts, Feelings, Images Coming Up?

Celebrate

Appreciate

Woohooo!!

Celebrate 10 Things! What Showed Up?

What Energy can I Be Today?

297:

Question

Ask

WWIT?

Today I'd like help with:

Questfirmation

Affirm

Why? How?

Questfirmations: Why? How?

Clear

Activate

De-Story, Transform Release

Any Thoughts, Feelings, Images Coming Up?

Celebrate

Appreciate

Woohooo!!

Celebrate 10 Things! What Showed Up?

What Energy can I Be Today?

298:

Question

Ask

WWIT?

Today I'd like help with:

Questfirmation

Affirm

Why? How?

Questfirmations: Why? How?

Clear

Activate

De-Story, Transform Release

Any Thoughts, Feelings, Images Coming Up?

Celebrate

Appreciate

Woohooo!!

Celebrate 10 Things! What Showed Up?

What Energy can I Be Today?

299:

Question

Ask

WWIT?

Today I'd like help with:

Questfirmation

Affirm

Why? How?

Questfirmations: Why? How?

Clear

Activate

De-Story, Transform Release

Any Thoughts, Feelings, Images Coming Up?

Celebrate

Appreciate

Woohooo!!

Celebrate 10 Things! What Showed Up?

What Energy can I Be Today?

300:

Question

Ask

WWIT?

Today I'd like help with:

Questfirmation

Affirm

Why? How?

Questfirmations: Why? How?

Clear

Activate

De-Story, Transform Release

Any Thoughts, Feelings, Images Coming Up?

Celebrate

Appreciate

Woohooo!!

Celebrate 10 Things! What Showed Up?

What Energy can I Be Today?

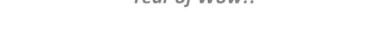

Home Stretch!! - Only 65 days left in your Year of Wow!!

Acknowledge, review and update!!

Still haven't reached some goals? Contact me to set up a
Complimentary Breakthrough Session -
info@attractmorenow.com

301:

Question

Ask

WWIT?

Today I'd like help with:

Questfirmation

Affirm

Why? How?

Questfirmations: Why? How?

Clear

Activate

De-Story, Transform
Release

Any Thoughts, Feelings, Images Coming Up?

Celebrate

Appreciate

Woohooo!!

Celebrate 10 Things! What Showed Up?

What Energy can I Be Today?

302:

Question

Ask

WWIT?

Today I'd like help with:

Questfirmation

Affirm

Why? How?

Questfirmations: Why? How?

Clear

Activate

De-Story, Transform Release

Any Thoughts, Feelings, Images Coming Up?

Celebrate

Appreciate

Woohooo!!

Celebrate 10 Things! What Showed Up?

What Energy can I Be Today?

303:

Question

Ask

WWIT?

Today I'd like help with:

Questfirmation

Affirm

Why? How?

Questfirmations: Why? How?

Clear

Activate

De-Story, Transform Release

Any Thoughts, Feelings, Images Coming Up?

Celebrate

Appreciate

Woohooo!!

Celebrate 10 Things! What Showed Up?

What Energy can I Be Today?

304:

Question

Ask

WWIT?

Today I'd like help with:

Questfirmation

Affirm

Why? How?

Questfirmations: Why? How?

Clear

Activate

De-Story, Transform Release

Any Thoughts, Feelings, Images Coming Up?

Celebrate

Appreciate

Woohooo!!

Celebrate 10 Things! What Showed Up?

What Energy can I Be Today?

305:

Question

Ask

WWIT?

Today I'd like help with:

Questfirmation

Affirm

Why? How?

Questfirmations: Why? How?

Clear

Activate

De-Story, Transform Release

Any Thoughts, Feelings, Images Coming Up?

Celebrate

Appreciate

Woohooo!!

Celebrate 10 Things! What Showed Up?

What Energy can I Be Today?

306:

Question

Ask
WWIT?

Today I'd like help with:

Questfirmation

Affirm
Why? How?

Questfirmations: Why? How?

Clear

Activate
De-Story, Transform
Release

Any Thoughts, Feelings, Images Coming Up?

Celebrate

Appreciate
Woohooo!!

Celebrate 10 Things! What Showed Up?

What Energy can I Be Today?

307:

Question

Ask
WWIT?

Today I'd like help with:

Questfirmation

Affirm
Why? How?

Questfirmations: Why? How?

Clear

Activate
De-Story, Transform Release

Any Thoughts, Feelings, Images Coming Up?

Celebrate

Appreciate
Woohooo!!

Celebrate 10 Things! What Showed Up?

What Energy can I Be Today?

308:

Question

Ask

WWIT?

Today I'd like help with:

Questfirmation

Affirm

Why? How?

Questfirmations: Why? How?

Clear

Activate

De-Story, Transform Release

Any Thoughts, Feelings, Images Coming Up?

Celebrate

Appreciate

Woohooo!!

Celebrate 10 Things! What Showed Up?

What Energy can I Be Today?

309:

Question

Ask
WWIT?

Today I'd like help with:

Questfirmation

Affirm
Why? How?

Questfirmations: Why? How?

Clear

Activate
De-Story, Transform Release

Any Thoughts, Feelings, Images Coming Up?

Celebrate

Appreciate
Woohooo!!

Celebrate 10 Things! What Showed Up?

What Energy can I Be Today?

310:

Question

Ask

WWIT?

Today I'd like help with:

Questfirmation

Affirm

Why? How?

Questfirmations: Why? How?

Clear

Activate

De-Story, Transform Release

Any Thoughts, Feelings, Images Coming Up?

Celebrate

Appreciate

Woohooo!!

Celebrate 10 Things! What Showed Up?

What Energy can I Be Today?

311:

Question

Ask

WWIT?

Today I'd like help with:

Questfirmation

Affirm

Why? How?

Questfirmations: Why? How?

Clear

Activate

De-Story, Transform
Release

Any Thoughts, Feelings, Images Coming Up?

Celebrate

Appreciate

Woohooo!!

Celebrate 10 Things! What Showed Up?

What Energy can I Be Today?

312:

Question

Ask
WWIT?

Today I'd like help with:

Questfirmation

Affirm
Why? How?

Questfirmations: Why? How?

Clear

Activate
De-Story, Transform Release

Any Thoughts, Feelings, Images Coming Up?

Celebrate

Appreciate
Woohooo!!

Celebrate 10 Things! What Showed Up?

What Energy can I Be Today?

313:

Question

Ask
WWIT?

Today I'd like help with:

Questfirmation

Affirm
Why? How?

Questfirmations: Why? How?

Clear

Activate
De-Story, Transform
Release

Any Thoughts, Feelings, Images Coming Up?

Celebrate

Appreciate
Woohooo!!

Celebrate 10 Things! What Showed Up?

What Energy can I Be Today?

314:

Question

Ask

WWIT?

Today I'd like help with:

Questfirmation

Affirm

Why? How?

Questfirmations: Why? How?

Clear

Activate

De-Story, Transform Release

Any Thoughts, Feelings, Images Coming Up?

Celebrate

Appreciate

Woohooo!!

Celebrate 10 Things! What Showed Up?

What Energy can I Be Today?

315:

Question

Ask
WWIT?

Today I'd like help with:

Questfirmation

Affirm
Why? How?

Questfirmations: Why? How?

Clear

Activate
De-Story, Transform
Release

Any Thoughts, Feelings, Images Coming Up?

Celebrate

Appreciate
Woohooo!!

Celebrate 10 Things! What Showed Up?

What Energy can I Be Today?

316:

Question

Ask

WWIT?

Today I'd like help with:

Questfirmation

Affirm

Why? How?

Questfirmations: Why? How?

Clear

Activate

**De-Story, Transform
Release**

Any Thoughts, Feelings, Images Coming Up?

Celebrate

Appreciate

Woohooo!!

Celebrate 10 Things! What Showed Up?

What Energy can I Be Today?

317:

Question

Ask

WWIT?

Today I'd like help with:

Questfirmation

Affirm

Why? How?

Questfirmations: Why? How?

Clear

Activate

De-Story, Transform Release

Any Thoughts, Feelings, Images Coming Up?

Celebrate

Appreciate

Woohooo!!

Celebrate 10 Things! What Showed Up?

What Energy can I Be Today?

318:

Ask

WWIT?

Today I'd like help with:

Questfirmation

Affirm

Why? How?

Questfirmations: Why? How?

Clear

Activate

De-Story, Transform Release

Any Thoughts, Feelings, Images Coming Up?

Celebrate

Appreciate

Woohooo!!

Celebrate 10 Things! What Showed Up?

What Energy can I Be Today?

319:

Question
Ask
WWIT?

Today I'd like help with:

Questfirmation
Affirm
Why? How?

Questfirmations: Why? How?

Clear
Activate
De-Story, Transform Release

Any Thoughts, Feelings, Images Coming Up?

Celebrate
Appreciate
Woohooo!!

Celebrate 10 Things! What Showed Up?

What Energy can I Be Today?

320:

Question

Ask
WWIT?

Today I'd like help with:

Questfirmation

Affirm
Why? How?

Questfirmations: Why? How?

Clear

Activate
**De-Story, Transform
Release**

Any Thoughts, Feelings, Images Coming Up?

Celebrate

Appreciate
Woohooo!!

Celebrate 10 Things! What Showed Up?

What Energy can I Be Today?

321:

Question

Ask
WWIT?

Today I'd like help with:

Questfirmation

Affirm
Why? How?

Questfirmations: Why? How?

Clear

Activate
De-Story, Transform Release

Any Thoughts, Feelings, Images Coming Up?

Celebrate

Appreciate
Woohooo!!

Celebrate 10 Things! What Showed Up?

What Energy can I Be Today?

322:

Question

Ask

WWIT?

Today I'd like help with:

Questfirmation

Affirm

Why? How?

Questfirmations: Why? How?

Clear

Activate

De-Story, Transform Release

Any Thoughts, Feelings, Images Coming Up?

Celebrate

Appreciate

Woohooo!!

Celebrate 10 Things! What Showed Up?

What Energy can I Be Today?

323:

Question

Ask

WWIT?

Today I'd like help with:

Questfirmation

Affirm

Why? How?

Questfirmations: Why? How?

Clear

Activate

De-Story, Transform Release

Any Thoughts, Feelings, Images Coming Up?

Celebrate

Appreciate

Woohooo!!

Celebrate 10 Things! What Showed Up?

What Energy can I Be Today?

324:

Question

Ask
WWIT?

Today I'd like help with:

Questfirmation

Affirm
Why? How?

Questfirmations: Why? How?

Clear

Activate
De-Story, Transform Release

Any Thoughts, Feelings, Images Coming Up?

Celebrate

Appreciate
Woohooo!!

Celebrate 10 Things! What Showed Up?

What Energy can I Be Today?

325:

Today I'd like help with:

Ask

WWIT?

Questfirmation

Questfirmations: Why? How?

Affirm

Why? How?

Clear

Any Thoughts, Feelings, Images Coming Up?

Activate

De-Story, Transform Release

Celebrate

Celebrate 10 Things! What Showed Up?

Appreciate

Woohooo!!

What Energy can I Be Today?

326:

Question

Ask

WWIT?

Today I'd like help with:

Questfirmation

Affirm

Why? How?

Questfirmations: Why? How?

Clear

Activate

De-Story, Transform Release

Any Thoughts, Feelings, Images Coming Up?

Celebrate

Appreciate

Woohooo!!

Celebrate 10 Things! What Showed Up?

What Energy can I Be Today?

327:

Question

Ask
WWIT?

Today I'd like help with:

Questfirmation

Affirm
Why? How?

Questfirmations: Why? How?

Clear

Activate
De-Story, Transform Release

Any Thoughts, Feelings, Images Coming Up?

Celebrate

Appreciate
Woohooo!!

Celebrate 10 Things! What Showed Up?

What Energy can I Be Today?

328:

Question

Ask

WWIT?

Today I'd like help with:

Questfirmation

Affirm

Why? How?

Questfirmations: Why? How?

Clear

Activate

De-Story, Transform Release

Any Thoughts, Feelings, Images Coming Up?

Celebrate

Appreciate

Woohooo!!

Celebrate 10 Things! What Showed Up?

What Energy can I Be Today?

329:

Question

Ask

WWIT?

Today I'd like help with:

Questfirmation

Affirm

Why? How?

Questfirmations: Why? How?

Clear

Activate

De-Story, Transform Release

Any Thoughts, Feelings, Images Coming Up?

Celebrate

Appreciate

Woohooo!!

Celebrate 10 Things! What Showed Up?

What Energy can I Be Today?

330:

Question

Ask
WWIT?

Today I'd like help with:

Questfirmation

Affirm
Why? How?

Questfirmations: Why? How?

Clear

Activate
De-Story, Transform Release

Any Thoughts, Feelings, Images Coming Up?

Celebrate

Appreciate
Woohooo!!

Celebrate 10 Things! What Showed Up?

What Energy can I Be Today?

331:

Question
Ask
WWIT?

Today I'd like help with:

Questfirmation
Affirm
Why? How?

Questfirmations: Why? How?

Clear
Activate
De-Story, Transform Release

Any Thoughts, Feelings, Images Coming Up?

Celebrate
Appreciate
Woohooo!!

Celebrate 10 Things! What Showed Up?

What Energy can I Be Today?

332:

Question

Ask
WWIT?

Today I'd like help with:

Questfirmation

Affirm
Why? How?

Questfirmations: Why? How?

Clear

Activate
De-Story, Transform Release

Any Thoughts, Feelings, Images Coming Up?

Celebrate

Appreciate
Woohooo!!

Celebrate 10 Things! What Showed Up?

What Energy can I Be Today?

333:

Question

Ask

WWIT?

Today I'd like help with:

Questfirmation

Affirm

Why? How?

Questfirmations: Why? How?

Clear

Activate

De-Story, Transform Release

Any Thoughts, Feelings, Images Coming Up?

Celebrate

Appreciate

Woohooo!!

Celebrate 10 Things! What Showed Up?

What Energy can I Be Today?

334:

Question

Ask
WWIT?

Today I'd like help with:

Questfirmation

Affirm
Why? How?

Questfirmations: Why? How?

Clear

Activate
De-Story, Transform Release

Any Thoughts, Feelings, Images Coming Up?

Celebrate

Appreciate
Woohooo!!

Celebrate 10 Things! What Showed Up?

What Energy can I Be Today?

335:

Question

Ask

WWIT?

Today I'd like help with:

Questfirmation

Affirm

Why? How?

Questfirmations: Why? How?

Clear

Activate

De-Story, Transform Release

Any Thoughts, Feelings, Images Coming Up?

Celebrate

Appreciate

Woohooo!!

Celebrate 10 Things! What Showed Up?

What Energy can I Be Today?

336:

Question

Ask

WWIT?

Today I'd like help with:

Questfirmation

Affirm

Why? How?

Questfirmations: Why? How?

Clear

Activate

De-Story, Transform Release

Any Thoughts, Feelings, Images Coming Up?

Celebrate

Appreciate

Woohooo!!

Celebrate 10 Things! What Showed Up?

What Energy can I Be Today?

337:

Question

Ask

WWIT?

Today I'd like help with:

Questfirmation

Affirm

Why? How?

Questfirmations: Why? How?

Clear

Activate

De-Story, Transform
Release

Any Thoughts, Feelings, Images Coming Up?

Celebrate

Appreciate

Woohooo!!

Celebrate 10 Things! What Showed Up?

What Energy can I Be Today?

338:

Question

Ask
WWIT?

Today I'd like help with:

Questfirmation

Affirm
Why? How?

Questfirmations: Why? How?

Clear

Activate
De-Story, Transform Release

Any Thoughts, Feelings, Images Coming Up?

Celebrate

Appreciate
Woohooo!!

Celebrate 10 Things! What Showed Up?

What Energy can I Be Today?

339:

Question

Ask
WWIT?

Today I'd like help with:

Questfirmation

Affirm
Why? How?

Questfirmations: Why? How?

Clear

Activate
De-Story, Transform
Release

Any Thoughts, Feelings, Images Coming Up?

Celebrate

Appreciate
Woohooo!!

Celebrate 10 Things! What Showed Up?

What Energy can I Be Today?

340:

Question

Ask
WWIT?

Today I'd like help with:

Questfirmation

Affirm
Why? How?

Questfirmations: Why? How?

Clear

Activate
De-Story, Transform Release

Any Thoughts, Feelings, Images Coming Up?

Celebrate

Appreciate
Woohooo!!

Celebrate 10 Things! What Showed Up?

What Energy can I Be Today?

341:

Question

Ask

WWIT?

Today I'd like help with:

Questfirmation

Affirm

Why? How?

Questfirmations: Why? How?

Clear

Activate

De-Story, Transform Release

Any Thoughts, Feelings, Images Coming Up?

Celebrate

Appreciate

Woohooo!!

Celebrate 10 Things! What Showed Up?

What Energy can I Be Today?

342:

Question

Ask

WWIT?

Today I'd like help with:

Questfirmation

Affirm

Why? How?

Questfirmations: Why? How?

Clear

Activate

De-Story, Transform Release

Any Thoughts, Feelings, Images Coming Up?

Celebrate

Appreciate

Woohooo!!

Celebrate 10 Things! What Showed Up?

What Energy can I Be Today?

343:

Question

Ask
WWIT?

Today I'd like help with:

Questfirmation

Affirm
Why? How?

Questfirmations: Why? How?

Clear

Activate
De-Story, Transform
Release

Any Thoughts, Feelings, Images Coming Up?

Celebrate

Appreciate
Woohooo!!

Celebrate 10 Things! What Showed Up?

What Energy can I Be Today?

344:

Question

Ask

WWIT?

Today I'd like help with:

Questfirmation

Affirm

Why? How?

Questfirmations: Why? How?

Clear

Activate

De-Story, Transform Release

Any Thoughts, Feelings, Images Coming Up?

Celebrate

Appreciate

Woohooo!!

Celebrate 10 Things! What Showed Up?

What Energy can I Be Today?

345:

Question

Ask
WWIT?

Today I'd like help with:

Questfirmation

Affirm
Why? How?

Questfirmations: Why? How?

Clear

Activate
De-Story, Transform
Release

Any Thoughts, Feelings, Images Coming Up?

Celebrate

Appreciate
Woohooo!!

Celebrate 10 Things! What Showed Up?

What Energy can I Be Today?

346:

Question

Ask

WWIT?

Today I'd like help with:

Questfirmation

Affirm

Why? How?

Questfirmations: Why? How?

Clear

Activate

De-Story, Transform Release

Any Thoughts, Feelings, Images Coming Up?

Celebrate

Appreciate

Woohooo!!

Celebrate 10 Things! What Showed Up?

What Energy can I Be Today?

347:

Question

Ask

WWIT?

Today I'd like help with:

Questfirmation

Affirm

Why? How?

Questfirmations: Why? How?

Clear

Activate

De-Story, Transform Release

Any Thoughts, Feelings, Images Coming Up?

Celebrate

Appreciate

Woohooo!!

Celebrate 10 Things! What Showed Up?

What Energy can I Be Today?

348:

Question

Ask

WWIT?

Today I'd like help with:

Questfirmation

Affirm

Why? How?

Questfirmations: Why? How?

Clear

Activate

De-Story, Transform Release

Any Thoughts, Feelings, Images Coming Up?

Celebrate

Appreciate

Woohooo!!

Celebrate 10 Things! What Showed Up?

What Energy can I Be Today?

349:

Question

Ask

WWIT?

Today I'd like help with:

Questfirmation

Affirm

Why? How?

Questfirmations: Why? How?

Clear

Activate

De-Story, Transform Release

Any Thoughts, Feelings, Images Coming Up?

Celebrate

Appreciate

Woohooo!!

Celebrate 10 Things! What Showed Up?

What Energy can I Be Today?

350:

Question

Ask

WWIT?

Today I'd like help with:

Questfirmation

Affirm

Why? How?

Questfirmations: Why? How?

Clear

Activate

De-Story, Transform Release

Any Thoughts, Feelings, Images Coming Up?

Celebrate

Appreciate

Woohooo!!

Celebrate 10 Things! What Showed Up?

What Energy can I Be Today?

351:

Question

Ask
WWIT?

Today I'd like help with:

Questfirmation

Affirm
Why? How?

Questfirmations: Why? How?

Clear

Activate
De-Story, Transform
Release

Any Thoughts, Feelings, Images Coming Up?

Celebrate

Appreciate
Woohooo!!

Celebrate 10 Things! What Showed Up?

What Energy can I Be Today?

352:

Question

Ask
WWIT?

Today I'd like help with:

Questfirmation

Affirm
Why? How?

Questfirmations: Why? How?

Clear

Activate
De-Story, Transform Release

Any Thoughts, Feelings, Images Coming Up?

Celebrate

Appreciate
Woohooo!!

Celebrate 10 Things! What Showed Up?

What Energy can I Be Today?

353:

Question
Ask
WWIT?

Today I'd like help with:

Questfirmation
Affirm
Why? How?

Questfirmations: Why? How?

Clear
Activate
De-Story, Transform Release

Any Thoughts, Feelings, Images Coming Up?

Celebrate
Appreciate
Woohooo!!

Celebrate 10 Things! What Showed Up?

What Energy can I Be Today?

354:

Question

Ask

WWIT?

Today I'd like help with:

Questfirmation

Affirm

Why? How?

Questfirmations: Why? How?

Clear

Activate

De-Story, Transform Release

Any Thoughts, Feelings, Images Coming Up?

Celebrate

Appreciate

Woohooo!!

Celebrate 10 Things! What Showed Up?

What Energy can I Be Today?

355:

Question

Ask

WWIT?

Today I'd like help with:

Questfirmation

Affirm

Why? How?

Questfirmations: Why? How?

Clear

Activate

De-Story, Transform Release

Any Thoughts, Feelings, Images Coming Up?

Celebrate

Appreciate

Woohooo!!

Celebrate 10 Things! What Showed Up?

What Energy can I Be Today?

356:

Question

Ask

WWIT?

Today I'd like help with:

Questfirmation

Affirm

Why? How?

Questfirmations: Why? How?

Clear

Activate

De-Story, Transform Release

Any Thoughts, Feelings, Images Coming Up?

Celebrate

Appreciate

Woohooo!!

Celebrate 10 Things! What Showed Up?

What Energy can I Be Today?

357:

Question

Ask

WWIT?

Today I'd like help with:

Questfirmation

Affirm

Why? How?

Questfirmations: Why? How?

Clear

Activate

De-Story, Transform Release

Any Thoughts, Feelings, Images Coming Up?

Celebrate

Appreciate

Woohooo!!

Celebrate 10 Things! What Showed Up?

What Energy can I Be Today?

358:

Question

Ask

WWIT?

Today I'd like help with:

Questfirmation

Affirm

Why? How?

Questfirmations: Why? How?

Clear

Activate

De-Story, Transform Release

Any Thoughts, Feelings, Images Coming Up?

Celebrate

Appreciate

Woohooo!!

Celebrate 10 Things! What Showed Up?

What Energy can I Be Today?

359:

Question

Ask

WWIT?

Today I'd like help with:

Questfirmation

Affirm

Why? How?

Questfirmations: Why? How?

Clear

Activate

De-Story, Transform Release

Any Thoughts, Feelings, Images Coming Up?

Celebrate

Appreciate

Woohooo!!

Celebrate 10 Things! What Showed Up?

What Energy can I Be Today?

360:

Question

Ask

WWIT?

Today I'd like help with:

Questfirmation

Affirm

Why? How?

Questfirmations: Why? How?

Clear

Activate

De-Story, Transform Release

Any Thoughts, Feelings, Images Coming Up?

Celebrate

Appreciate

Woohooo!!

Celebrate 10 Things! What Showed Up?

What Energy can I Be Today?

361:

Question

Ask

WWIT?

Today I'd like help with:

Questfirmation

Affirm

Why? How?

Questfirmations: Why? How?

Clear

Activate

De-Story, Transform Release

Any Thoughts, Feelings, Images Coming Up?

Celebrate

Appreciate

Woohooo!!

Celebrate 10 Things! What Showed Up?

What Energy can I Be Today?

362:

Question

Ask

WWIT?

Today I'd like help with:

Questfirmation

Affirm

Why? How?

Questfirmations: Why? How?

Clear

Activate

De-Story, Transform Release

Any Thoughts, Feelings, Images Coming Up?

Celebrate

Appreciate

Woohooo!!

Celebrate 10 Things! What Showed Up?

What Energy can I Be Today?

363:

Question

Ask

WWIT?

Today I'd like help with:

Questfirmation

Affirm

Why? How?

Questfirmations: Why? How?

Clear

Activate

De-Story, Transform Release

Any Thoughts, Feelings, Images Coming Up?

Celebrate

Appreciate

Woohooo!!

Celebrate 10 Things! What Showed Up?

What Energy can I Be Today?

364:

Question

Ask

WWIT?

Today I'd like help with:

Questfirmation

Affirm

Why? How?

Questfirmations: Why? How?

Clear

Activate

De-Story, Transform Release

Any Thoughts, Feelings, Images Coming Up?

Celebrate

Appreciate

Woohooo!!

Celebrate 10 Things! What Showed Up?

What Energy can I Be Today?

365:

Question

Ask

WWIT?

Today I'd like help with:

Questfirmation

Affirm

Why? How?

Questfirmations: Why? How?

Clear

Activate

De-Story, Transform
Release

Any Thoughts, Feelings, Images Coming Up?

Celebrate

Appreciate

Woohooo!!

Celebrate 10 Things! What Showed Up?

What Energy can I Be Today?

How to Reach Us

**No Matter Where You Are,
Karen Can Help You Attract What You Want!**

If you would like more information about how Karen Luniw or her team can help you or your organization, please visit **www.AttractMoreNow.com**.

There you will find information on a variety of Karen's program including:

- Coaching Programs
- Workshops and Teleseminars
- Speaking opportunities

You can speed up your progress and break down your blocks to what you want quicker by working with Karen directly or in one of her programs.

To connect with Karen and her team today, please just drop an email to info@AttractMoreNow.com or call and leave a message at 250 808-5628 (Canada/International) 310 256-2305 (US) and we will get back to you shortly.

Don't see what you're looking for? Contact us!

About Karen Luniw

Karen Luniw & Attract More Now burst into life with the advent of podcasting in 2006. Karen's podcast *'Law of Attraction Tips'* has been in the Top 10 on iTunes Self-Help Section for 6 years and has accumulated a whopping 20 million plus downloads in that time.

Karen Luniw is a Mindset Expert specializing in helping Executives and Entrepreneurs to have more time and money. She is the author *'Attraction in Action: Your How to Guide to Relationships, Money, Work and Health'* and forthcoming book *'Questfirmations'*, is a contributor to The Huffington Post and has been featured in the Vancouver Sun, the Financial Post and as a guest on radio and TV.

Smart, driven Executives & Entrepreneurs with personal and business mindset challenges from all over the world come to her to attract more from life and business. Because Karen's background has been in business and employment it was natural for her to attract people from all walks of life including stay at home Moms to Hollywood creatives to people who work in the Executive Office of the President of the United States. Essentially, Karen helps Conscious-Minded people to Shift. Align. Shine. Shift their perspectives and beliefs. Align with their Dreams. Shine their Light in the World. She teaches how to use a new mindset and other powerful tools to achieve goals smarter and faster through her speaking events, coaching and products.

Made in the USA
Charleston, SC
09 October 2014